Sea Kayak

Around
Vancouver
Island

Doug Alderson

Rocky
Mountain Books
Calgary–Victoria–Vancouver

Front cover: Morning on South Brooks Peninsula.

All photos by author unless otherwise indicated.

We acknowledge the financial support of the Government of Canada through the Book Publishing Industry Development Program (BPIDP) and the support of the Alberta Foundation for the Arts for our publishing program.

Copyright © 2004 Doug Alderson

Printed in Canada

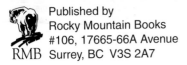
Published by
Rocky Mountain Books
#106, 17665-66A Avenue
RMB   Surrey, BC V3S 2A7

National Library of Canada Cataloguing in Publication

Alderson, Doug
   Sea kayak around Vancouver Island / Doug Alderson.

Includes index.
ISBN 1-894765-50-8

   1. Sea kayaking--British Columbia--Vancouver Island--Guidebooks.
2. Vancouver Island (B.C.)--Guidebooks. I. Title.

GV776.15.B7A42 2004   797.1'224'097112
C2004-900731-9

Contents

Paddling Areas

Preface

For he will find at sea the full model of human life;
that is if he sails on his own in a little craft
suitable to the little stature of one man.
The Cruise of The Nona by Hilaire Belloc

For the First Peoples of Vancouver Island the canoe was a means of practical and spiritual transportation. The dugout canoe, once a living tree and host to a community of plants and animals, took on a second life as a vessel for a community of people. In the past, the canoe and kayak were more than mere tools for subsistence. Beyond their utilitarian use for the hunter-gatherer, independent travel by kayak or any small boat was a metaphor for life and spirit. Although the modern sea kayak is designed differently and made of different materials, it remains a means of human powered transportation. The simple practice of pulling the boat forward, one paddle stroke at a time, with uncomplicated human effort, has not changed. All paddlers share in this experience. Today the primary purpose of paddling has changed from subsistence to recreation, but paddling as a means for spiritual transportation remains relevant.

About this Book

The route described in this book starts at the foot of a little wooden bridge across the entrance to Esquimalt Lagoon in Victoria and continues counterclockwise around Vancouver Island. Where you choose to start is of course entirely up to you. I chose this place because here, as a child, I built a raft of driftwood logs and began a journey of paddling around Vancouver Island. Here too, is where the beacon of Fisgard Lighthouse beckons all sea travellers to return home safely.

It is my hope that the contents of this guidebook will be used to suit individual needs. This is, in fact, my experience: wandering here and there in search of the most beautiful beach, the bluest wave, the most diverse wildlife and the friendship of those unique individuals who choose to live along the shores of an island.

Diagrams provided in this book are intended as guidance in planning a trip; you will require all the necessary marine charts to navigate the shore, and road maps and accommodation guides to get you to the launch site and back.

Because a considerable amount of information is needed to plan a trip, it would be unjust to offer all the necessary details in only a few short paragraphs. There is a section of reference material in the appendix that attempts to do justice to this substantial body of knowledge. My book "Sea Kayaker Magazine's Handbook of Safety and Rescue" was written with these topics in mind.

Directions and Distances

- All compass and cardinal directions are given as True.
- All sea distance are given in nautical miles.
- All land distances are given in kilometers.

Conversion Factors

nmi x 1.85 = km
nmi x 1.15 = statute mile (mi)
statute mile x 1.16 = km
statute mile x 0.87 = nm
km x 0.54 = nmi
km x 0.62 = stat mile

Key to Icons

⊠ hazard (refer to text for description)
⌘ point of interest
⌂ camping – fees may apply
≋ fresh water available (boil before drinking)
↗ water taxi service available
⚓ road access to this site (includes car ferries)
◆ groceries and supplies available

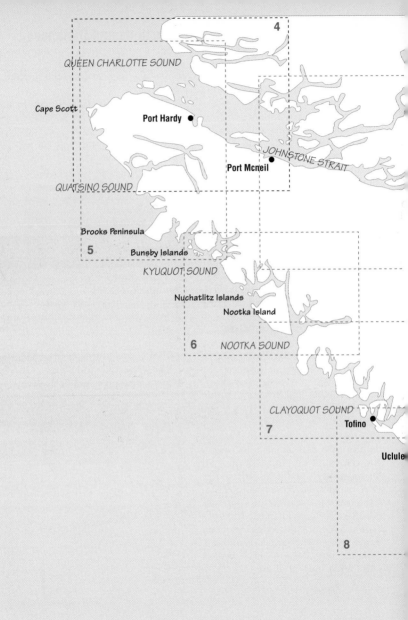

QUEEN CHARLOTTE SOUND

4

Cape Scott

Port Hardy

JOHNSTONE STRAIT

Port Mcneil

QUATSINO SOUND

Brooks Peninsula

5

Bunsby Islands

KYUQUOT SOUND

Nuchatlitz Islands

Nootka Island

6   NOOTKA SOUND

CLAYOQUOT SOUND

7   Tofino

Uclule

8

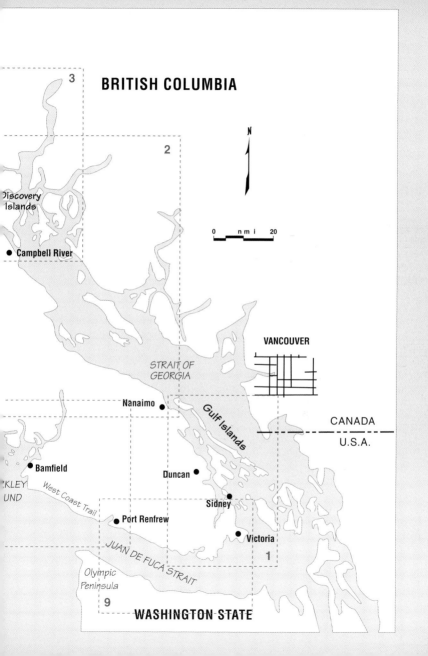

Vancouver Island

Vancouver Island is incredibly diverse and full of surprises. Nobody could ever know it all, but it is a place that invites the attempt.

The Unknown Island by Ian Smith

The earliest known evidence of habitation on Vancouver Island dates to about 5,000 years ago. An abundance of clean water, berries, fish and game provided ample food, and timber and cedar bark were used as materials for building canoes and creating art. Unfortunately, the forest has consumed many relics of the past. Totem poles, long houses, magnificent ocean-going canoes, cedar bark clothing, and utensils for daily use have been largely recycled into the environment. The first responsibility of the sea kayaker touring these shores is to follow that example and leave nothing behind.

At 32,137 square kilometres, Vancouver Island is the largest island off W North America. It is 460 km long and 50 to 130 kilometres wide with an intricate coastline of more than 3,000 kilometres. The Island's population of 600,000 is concentrated along the east coast with only sparse settlement and few roads on the west coast.

The island is separated from continental British Columbia by Queen Charlotte Strait, Johnstone Strait, Strait of Georgia, and Juan de Fuca Strait.

Environmental regions

Complex geography divides the island into four general environmental zones.

Southeastern Zone
Victoria to Campbell River

The coastline from Victoria to Campbell River is dominated by an archipelago of islands and a coastal plain free of large inlets. Between Vancouver Island and the continental mainland is a passage replete with islands and sheltered coves. The southwest is the most populated portion of Vancouver Island comprising more than 90% of the population. Victoria is the province's capital with a metropolitan population of 300,000.

The Olympic Peninsula near Victoria and the southern Gulf Islands, provides shelter from the worst of marine weather, and weather in the region is typically moderate and dry, almost Mediterranean in character. Farther north the mountainous spine of Vancouver Island provides similar shelter to the northern reaches of the Strait of Georgia.

As the tide floods into the Juan de Fuca Strait and turns the corner to the Strait of Georgia where complex currents bring up deeper cold water keeping the surface a chilly 9 °C throughout most of the year. In the northern reaches of the Strait of Georgia there is a tidal doldrum where the incoming tide from the north meets the incoming tide from the south. These are the world famous cruising waters of Desolation Sound. In summer the water temperature in a few isolated bays can exceed 20 °C.

The cold southern currents encourage rich marine ecosystems. Birds, fish, seals, sea lion and resident pods of killer whales are always close by. The warmer still waters in the north enable the growth of large oyster beds and commercial harvesting.

Northeastern Zone
Campbell River to Cape Scott

The city of Campbell River (population 30,000) marks the north end of the Strait of Georgia. At this point there is a dramatic change in geography and weather. A dense, near impenetrable, evergreen forest reaches down to the water's edge with the lower branches touching the highest tides. Moisture-laden weather coming in from the northwest is funneled into Queen Charlotte Strait and through Johnstone Strait. Considerable rain falls along the steep mountainsides. The continental shoreline in places is only two miles away and scoured with steep inlets that cut tens of miles deep into the British Columbia mainland. In winter, cold continental weather systems spill their cold winds out of these mainland inlets.

The minimal currents in northern Strait of Georgia are contrasted by nasty 12 to 16 knot tidal rapids on either side of Quadra Island. Once through the labyrinth of whirlpools and overfalls surrounding Quadra Island, the narrow length of Johnstone Strait funnels both wind and current into close alignment. Frequent gales blowing against ebb currents of three to five knots create particularly poor sea conditions.

Salmon returning to spawn up the rivers of continental BC and Vancouver Island are funneled into Johnstone Strait. With the salmon come killer whales. Both resident and transient pods of whales circulate through the waters of Johnstone Strait to feed and socialize. Here is the largest concentration of killer whales in the world with occasional super-pods of up to 50 animals or more. On shore black bears scour the rivers and beaches for nutritious remains of spawning salmon.

Near the northernmost extremity of Vancouver Island is Port Hardy (population 5,200), the last stop before the very sparsely populated west coast. The next towns accessible by road, Gold River or Tofino, are 180 and 220 miles around to the southeast both with populations of about 1,500.

Northwestern Zone
Cape Scott to Tofino

The northwest coast is exposed to the full intensity of the Pacific Ocean. The magnificently rugged coastline is punctuated by stunning surf-swept beaches. Several inlets cut into the coast providing marginal reprieve from the brunt of incoming weather. The heavy rainfall and violent windstorms of the Cape Scott area are legendary. Annual rainfall is between 375 and 500 centimeters. Even in summer, prolonged sunny periods are rare. Once you have rounded the blunt western exposure of Cape Cook on Brooks Peninsula the weather moderates steadily as you travel south.

All along the west coast, moderate temperatures and high precipitation combine to produce a long growing period that supports a lush temperate rainforest. On exposed headlands, wind-sheared low growth, evidence of steady winter gales, is backed by a temperate rain forest of giant cedar, hemlock and Sitka spruce standing over dense undergrowth. Cedars hundreds of years, old, stressed by harsh conditions, have developed twisted, split trunks and gray deadwood spires. This old-growth temperate rainforest is known as one of the highest biomass-producing areas in the world. A tangle of dark green salal provides a nearly impassible barrier between the forest and the beach.

Large mammals use beaches as a transportation corridor and signs of cougar, wolf and black bear are common. The cold clean water provides for an intertidal zone rich with kelp, fish, clams, abalone, crabs and tide pool invertebrates. In the kelp beds offshore, sea otters, seals, sea lions, killer, humpback and grey whales and porpoise are the sea kayakers' regular companions. A wide range of seabirds are found in the area including bald eagles, osprey, ravens, oystercatchers, cormorants, auklets and many others.

Southwestern Zone
Tofino to Victoria

This southwestern coast provides exciting and accessible sea kayaking for all interests including sunbathing, surfing, exploring sections of rugged open coast or investigating miles of sheltered sounds and complex shoreline. To provide shipwrecked sailors a route to civilization, the world famous West Coast Trail was hacked through the dense forest along a shoreline of shallow shelving rock and beach.

Clayoquot Sound and Barkley Sound are world-renowned sea-kayaking destinations. Although sparsely populated, the influx of tourists into small towns such as Tofino, Ucluelet and Bamfield make them very busy during the summer months.

Juan de Fuca Strait is formed by Vancouver Island to the northeast and the Olympic Mountains of Washington State to the southwest. The straight uninterrupted coastlines create a funnel for daily thermal winds, which during the summer, blow strong on most afternoons.

Race Rock is a tiny ecological reserve protecting a unique balance of shelter and exposure. A picturesque black-and-white banded lighthouse marks the current sweep tidal race that gives Race Rock its name. Ten miles from Victoria this tiny piece of isolated rock is a haul-out for harbour seals, California sea lions, Stellar's sea lion, elephant seals (there was once a northern fur seal here for several seasons). Colonies of nesting seabirds are supported by a rich subtidal community.

Planning Considerations

Guidelines for Planning Travel Times

I have found that over the years a few general timelines apply to most of my trips. Although a two-day trip for one paddler may be a weeklong trip for another, the travelling days are often similar.

On a coastal trip I average 15 miles per travelling day. A typical day is 1.5 hours to break camp, 2.5 hours paddling, 1 hour for lunch, 2.5 hours paddling, 1.5 hours to make camp, 1 hour for dinner. That is a 10-hour day.

On the open coast, I allow one day in three to be held up for bad weather. I like to break camp and travel every second day. So, six days of travelling may take up six campsites for two nights each and two days held up for weather—it could be as long as a 14-day trip. Making the most general plans in this way, I have been able to accommodate most situations, staying longer in the finest of campsites, moving on more frequently when I am restless and paddling longer days when I feel energetic. When gales keep me shore-bound, I have the time to wait for calmer seas.

On trips that have the transiting of distance as a primary purpose, I still make a rough plan for an average 15 miles per day and one day in three ashore for bad weather. Rest days fit into this schedule at the expense of some 20- or 25-mile paddling days. In this way, I have often been home a couple days early, but so far, I have never returned a couple days late.

Judging the Risks

Adventures are nasty disturbing uncomfortable things that make you late for dinner. Bilbo Baggins in *The Hobbit.*

While experience may be the best teacher the cost of mistakes can be very high. Taking courses in paddling skills and seamanship is a good beginning as is travelling in the company of competent leaders. Local knowledge and awareness is also key to a successful trip along a demanding coastline.

Practicing rescue skills is part of preparing for a trip.

Trip Rating

Under "Paddling Conditions," you will find recommended areas for beginner, intermediate and advanced paddlers that have been rated according to the paddling skills required, normal sea and shoreline conditions and the risk normally associated with such conditions. The rating given to an area is an indication of what to expect in good, summer conditions. It is an assessment of risk, taking into account paddling skills and difficulties likely to be encountered.

Difficulty is a measure of sea conditions: wind, waves, currents, tide rips and length of open–water crossings and shoreline conditions: surf and infrequent and/or difficult landings.

Risk is the possibility of inconvenience, discomfort, injury or even loss of life. For the paddler, the level of risk is not constant. Along the same route and with the same paddling conditions, different paddlers will encounter different levels of risk. For a beginner, risky conditions may include small wavelets that arise before white–capped waves appear. For a more skilled paddler the same waves may hardly be noticeable. Risk can be reduced by good paddling skills, knowledge and judgement. Risk is increased in worsening conditions, remote locations and with poor decision–making.

There is a complex relationship between paddling skills, difficulty and risk. The individual paddler's skill level, the nature of the route, changing weather, and the presence of a competent leader are essential factors in determining the difficulty and risk of a sea kayak journey.

Sound decision–making is critical to the enjoyment and safety of sea kayaking touring, and an experienced leader will often reduce difficulty and risk to acceptable levels. In the company of a skilled leader, a beginner paddler can paddle safely along a coast rated intermediate. With good leadership a large portion of the Island's coastline is accessible to beginner–level paddlers, and a coastline rated as advanced is by no means the sole domain of the advanced paddler.

The rating descriptions below cover many, but not all, of the factors required to assess difficulty and risk. There may be other factors to be considered such as river outflows, reflected waves, the profile of a surf beach, and limitations of gear and cold water.

The skill levels referred to below correspond to the conditions i.e. intermediate paddlers have the attributes necessary to safely travel in intermediate conditions.

Novice conditions – minimal risk
- Sheltered locations with stable conditions.
- Wind calm (less than 8 knots); sea state calm to rippled.
- Travel is along shore with abundant easy landing sites.
- Frequent opportunities for communication and road access; assistance is nearby.

A group of novice paddlers can travel safely on day trips along the shore. Poor decisions or misinterpreting changing weather or sea conditions is unlikely to cause harm or significant inconvenience.

Beginner conditions – low risk
- Mostly sheltered locations with stable conditions.
- Light winds (0–11 knots) current (0–0.5 knots) Sea state calm to light chop.
- Abundant easy landing sites and short open crossings less than 1.5 nmi.
- Frequent opportunities for communication and access; assistance may be up to an hour away.

A group of beginners can travel safely on day trips. Intermediate paddlers familiar with the area could lead beginners on an overnight trip. Poor decisions or misinterpreting changing weather or sea conditions is likely to cause inconvenience but unlikely to cause harm.

Intermediate conditions – moderate risk
- A complex open water environment with the potential for moderate change in conditions.
- Moderate winds (12–19 knots); sea state moderate with wind waves near 0.5 meters; surf less than 1 meter; current less than 3 knots.
- Intermittent landing opportunities with some difficult landing sites; open water crossings less than 5 nmi.
- Communication may be interrupted; assistance may be more than one hour away.

A group of intermediate paddlers can travel safely on day trips. Advanced paddlers familiar with the area could lead intermediate paddlers on an extended overnight trip. Poor decisions or misinterpreting changing weather or sea conditions is likely to cause great inconvenience, the need for external rescue and possibly personal harm.

Advanced conditions – considerable risk
- Complex open water environment with frequently changing conditions.
- Continuous exposure to wind, swell or current.
- Strong winds (near 20 knots); sea state rough with wind waves near 1 metre; surf greater than 1 metre or tide rips greater than 3 knots are routine.
- Infrequent landing opportunities with some difficult landing sites; open water crossings greater than 5 nmi
- Remote locations where communications can be difficult or unavailable; assistance may be a day or more away.

A mix of intermediate and advanced paddlers can travel safely on day trips. On extended overnight trips all paddlers should have advanced skills. Poor decisions or misinterpreting changing weather or sea conditions is likely to cause personal harm, without the availability of prompt external rescue.

Marine Weather

Knowledge and awareness of the weather is crucial to the safety and enjoyment of all sea kayaking activities. At sea, there is no shelter, yet the greatest risks are near the shore. A kayaker's refuge is a campsite on an exposed beach. Understanding the fundamentals of weather systems helps us interpret weather information.

Marine Weather Broadcasts

Continuous marine weather broadcasts are available on VHF radio channels WX 1–10. Weather forecasts predict patterns over large areas. Forecasts for a large area exhibit local inconsistencies because local geography alters the timing and intensity of the weather systems. A marine weather broadcast at 10 am may give you a weather report at Pachena Lighthouse at 4 am, the position of a trough of low pressure 50 miles to the northwest at 8 am, and a forecast for an area of 1,500 square miles from 9 am today untill 9 am tomorrow with an outlook for an additional 24 hours. The weather in your location may differ from all of these. It is an important to make sense of the scale, timing and severity of all this information.

Environment Canada updates its marine weather broadcasts 4 times each day and they can be heard continuously on VHF radio frequencies. Copies of these forecast are available over the phone and on the internet. These marine weather broadcasts reflect the diversity of the various environmental regions around Vancouver Island. There are distinct broadcasts for west coast Vancouver Island North, west coast Vancouver Island South, Juan de Fuca Strait, Haro Strait, Strait of Georgia, Johnstone Strait and Queen Charlotte Sound. See map on pages 16 and 17.

The local AM or FM radio station will announce local weather, and the road conditions to your launch site. The marine report will give you wind speed and direction and wave heights. At the dock, an angler could probably tell you about the effects of a north wind at the nearby headland. Listen to the weather reports and forecast for the wide-ranging weather information. For local weather effects look up and out to sea.

Weather Systems

High-pressure systems are associated with clear summer weather. During a high-pressure system, the strongest winds occur at the outer edges of the system where the air has had a chance to pick up speed. As a high approaches and passes overhead, the wind shifts clockwise (veers). A veering wind is generally associated with improving weather. During periods of good, warm weather, afternoon northwesterly winds can reach gale force.

Low-pressure weather systems are associated with low cloud cover, rain and wind. Wind flows counterclockwise and inward. As a system arrives, the winds shift counterclockwise (backs). With a low-pressure systems, the winds are strongest nearest the center. Typically, low-pressure systems have a wedge of warm air trapped between masses of cold

Fog on the beach at Nels Bight, Cape Scott.

air. The fronts associated with lows have characteristic wind and cloud patterns that can be recognized from the ground.

As a typical low approaches, the observer on the ground experiences cool temperatures, increasing cloud cover and a lowering cloud ceiling. A distinct warming and veering in wind direction indicates the arrival of the warm front. The wedge of warmer air is a sign of worse weather to follow. The strongest winds can be predicted to be behind the impending cold front. An observer near the center of the system will have very little time to take shelter and a sudden and severe change in weather can be forecast. Farther out from the center, the distance between the warm front and the cold front is greater, and there is more time to respond to a less severe change in the weather.

Fog is a common hazard along the west coast of Vancouver Island. In summer, steady northwest winds cause upwelling of cool water near shore. Moisture in warm wind blowing over the cool water condenses and forms marine fog. Fog can persist for days, but in most cases will dissipate by mid to late afternoon.

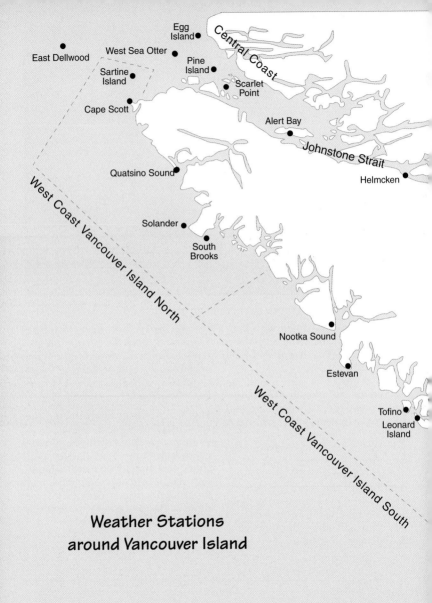

East Dellwood

Egg Island

Central Coast

West Sea Otter

Pine Island

Sartine Island

Scarlet Point

Cape Scott

Alert Bay

Johnstone Strait

Quatsino Sound

Helmcken

Solander

South Brooks

West Coast Vancouver Island North

Nootka Sound

Estevan

West Coast Vancouver Island South

Tofino

Leonard Island

Weather Stations
around Vancouver Island

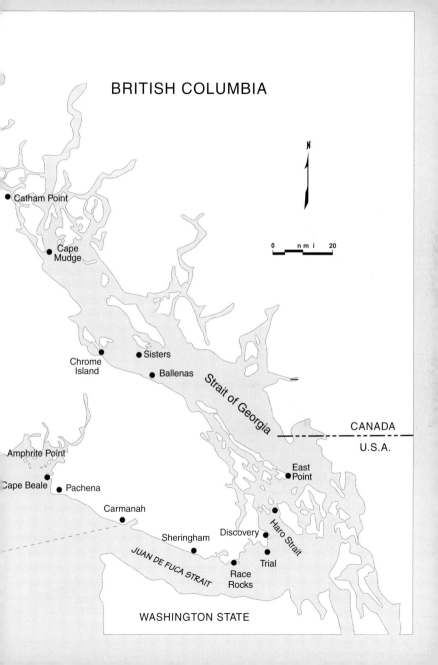

BRITISH COLUMBIA

N

0   n m i   20

Catham Point

Cape
Mudge

Sisters

Chrome
Island

Ballenas

Strait of Georgia

CANADA

U.S.A.

Amphrite Point

East
Point

Cape Beale

Pachena

Carmanah

Discovery

Haro Strait

Sheringham

Trial

JUAN DE FUCA STRAIT

Race
Rocks

WASHINGTON STATE

Tides and Currents

Understanding tidal currents is of fundamental importance when you are in a slow moving sea kayak. A well-planned trip should take full advantage of the positive effects of tidal currents and avoid its hazards.

Complex coastal geography dramatically alters the regular pattern of the tides. The patterns of tidal currents throughout the inland waterways of Vancouver Island are particularly complex and defy simple prediction. It is wrong to assume that a direct relationship exists between the rise and fall of the tide and flow of the current. Typically, kayakers are most attracted to irregular coastlines, which is where tidal current is exaggerated and complicated. Tidal current will usually reverse direction four times in a day, creating significant and complex changes in the sea state. In some locations, unique geography can produce a steady, uni-directional current during the rise and fall of the tide. This non-intuitive flow may occur infrequently during the monthly tidal cycle. Most often running at two to five knots at a maximum, tidal current can, in extreme cases, run in excess of 16 knots, standing waves reach three metres tall and create whirlpools that are 20 metres across with one metre-wide voids at their center. These rare and isolated extreme areas are well documented in the "Tide and Current Tables," the "Small Craft Guide" and marine charts.

For southern waters, the tidal current velocities and directions are predicted in "*Current Atlas: Juan de Fuca to Strait of Georgia*" published by Canadian Hydrographic Services. This atlas provides useful information, but the sea kayaker must still look over the edge of the kayak to observe the reality of the moment. The predominant flow in a main channel will predictably follow the tide data. However, the kayaks diminutive size and shallow draft allows it to navigate passages smaller than the data provided by tables and atlases.

Surge Narrows flowing at one-quarter of maximum. I was able to ferry across before it became any stronger.

Land Jurisdictions

First Nations Territories

The First Nations people of Vancouver Island are generally considered to be three ethnographically distinct peoples, the Coast Salish, the Nuu-chah-nulth (Nootka), the Kwakwaka'wakw (Kwakiutl).

Traditionally, the Coast Salish inhabited the coast from Johnstone Straight south and west to Port San Juan (Port Renfrew) and vast areas of western Washington State. The Nuu-chah-nulth (Nootka) territory covered the western coastline of Vancouver Island from Cape Scott south to Port Renfrew. The Kwakwaka'wakw region comprised the northeastern coastal tip of Vancouver Island from Cape Scott to Campbell River and the neighbouring mainland.

Each of these ethnographic groups consisted of many sub-groups and language dialects. Of the great many Indian reserves along the shores of Vancouver Island, some are busy villages, while others are inhabited only in summer and others are isolated beaches that are seldom visited at all. Indian reserves are clearly indicted on marine charts and topographical maps.

After more than 150 years of colonial occupation, the First Nations peoples of Vancouver Island continue to deal with land claims. Historically, the B.C. government did not recognize aboriginal land titles and so B.C. has few land treaties. In recent decades there has been a growing public and legal recognition of aboriginal rights and the provincial government has entered a long and difficult process of land claim negotiations that will continue well into the future.

The entire coastline of Vancouver Island and the adjacent small islands are home to many different groups of First Nations peoples. Areas designated as IR (Indian Reserves) on charts have restricted access. Local bands are usually cooperative and supportive of shared use of their lands, but you must obtain permission from the appropriate Indian Band office to land or camp. Many locations outside of designated

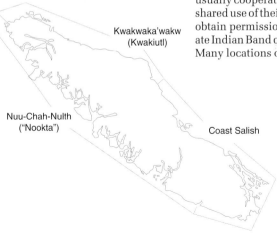

Kwakwaka'wakw
(Kwakiutl)

Nuu-Chah-Nulth
("Nookta")

Coast Salish

reserves contain scared burial sites, artifacts and other culturally sensitive materials. The spirit of no-trace camping is a good one to follow; leave untouched all materials presumed to be culturally significant.

Provincial Parks and Recreation Sites

Stewardship of BC Provincial parkland is changing. In 2003, the provincial Forest Service, along with volunteer groups, maintained about 600 recreation sites and 140 trails. However, by March 31, 2004, the government will no longer manage recreation sites and trails. Other parties will be sought out to take on the responsibilities. The outcome of this change of management is unknown at this time. In general, where fees are to be collected, there may be a self-pay strongbox or someone will come by to collect fees, usually in the early evening. For further details on park fees, go to the BC Parks home page at wlapwww.gov.bc.ca/bcparks/.

National Parks

Pacific Rim National Park, located on the west coast of Vancouver Island is managed by the federal government and encompasses 49,962 hectares of land and ocean in three separate geographic units: Long Beach; the Broken Group Islands; and the West Coast Trail. Park use fees, parking fees and camping fees vary throughout the park.

Within the park lie impressive rainforest and rich marine ecosystems. For thousands of years, the Nuu-chah-nulth First Nations inhabited this area, features of which include long sandy beaches, an island archipelago, old-growth coastal temperate rainforest and significant Nuu-chah-nulth archaeological sites.

The newly created Gulf Islands National Park is found in the southeastern quadrant of Vancouver Island and encompasses many Provincial marine parks. The participation of the federal government marks the beginning of land acquisition to expand and rationalize the park holdings. It remains to be seen how this park will be developed and managed in the

Choosing a Campsite

The quality of available campsites is an important consideration for safe and comfortable sea kayak touring. The weary paddler comes ashore at the end of the day, often wet and cold, still to contend with all the difficulties of setting up camp. The campsites available are often windy, taking the initial impact of stormy weather arriving onshore. In times of fair weather and neap tides, a tiny shell beach in a cove is an idyllic private campsite for a sea kayaker. In high winds and spring tides, the same site might be uncomfortable or dangerous.

In summer, high tide is in the middle of the night. During spring tides a good campsite at midday may be awash at midnight. Over the seasons and over the years, waves and tides reshape the beach and beachfront tent sites change; a beach berm a metre above high water one year can be a centimeter below water the next year.

- When possible, use parks and designated recreational areas.
- Choose a tent site high enough above sea level to avoid the highest possible tide. Stormy weather can substantially raise sea level and river levels can rise in only hours. In storm winds, falling tree branches and blowing sand can be hazardous.
- Inspect the area for signs of wildlife: tracks, droppings, overturned rocks, rotten trees torn apart, clawed, bitten or rubbed trees, or wildlife trails.
- Avoid camping near wildlife trails (usually at the ends of the beach).
- Tie down all kayaks; securely store all paddles and PFD's.

Minimum Impact

An increasing number of sea kayakers has increased pressure on campsites. To ensure the high quality of our wilderness experiences we must minimize our impact on the environment. When camp is broken no sign of human use should be left behind. While the phrase no trace camping is politically correct, it is not possible. If we walk along the intertidal zone, we crush periwinkles, shellfish and vegetation. Fortunately, this ecological zone can recover quickly. On shore, the evidence of a tent placed on a mossy knoll may last for years. There is little or no pristine wilderness remaining—our footsteps are evident in most places. Established park campsites or camping areas should be used where available. Put up your tent on the tent pads or cleared areas provided and use a backpacking stove for cooking rather than an open fire.

In some location there needs to be consideration to allow some non-designated camp areas to recover from over use. At least, avoid increasing the footprint of sensitive sites. Keep open fires to a minimum and do not create fire rings with rocks. Consider leaving your trace by removing evidence of prior less considerate campers. Where possible camp on the beach, not the upland. This is particularly important in areas of high use, sensitive ecosystems or archeological sites.

Human Excrement

Sea kayakers travelling along a wilderness coastline tend to land in the same places. If there are no available toilet facilities (usually pit toilets), the intertidal zone is the best place to deposit human feces. If depositing feces in the upland area, dig a small in the biologically active upper layer of soil, deposit the feces in the hole and cover with the removed soil. Toilet paper is best disposed of by burning.

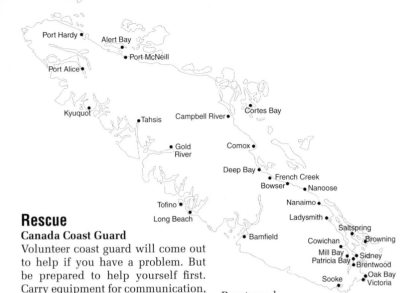

Rescue
Canada Coast Guard
Volunteer coast guard will come out to help if you have a problem. But be prepared to help yourself first. Carry equipment for communication, warmth, and floatation. Call sooner rather than later to facilitate a successful rescue and place your rescuers at minimal risk. Do not wait until the weather is at its strongest and you are at your weakest.

Specialized search and rescue craft are available at the locations shown on the map.

Canada Coast Guard Stations
Tofino
Bamfield
French Creek
Ganges
Victoria
Port Hardy
Campbell River

Coast Guard Volunteer Units
Alert Bay
Bamfield
Bowser
Brentwood
Browning Harbour
Campbell River
Comox
Cortes Bay
Cowichan
Gold River
Sidney
Kyuquot
Ladysmith
Long Beach
Mill Bay
Nanaimo
Nanoose
Oak bay
Patricia Bay
Port Alberni
Port Alice
Port McNeill
Powell River
Sooke
Tahsis
Victoria

Safety Considerations

Marine Traffic

Rules of the road and rights of way for marine traffic are written with larger, more visible craft in mind. The low profile and non-existent radar signal of a sea kayak make it vulnerable. Therefore, assume you cannot be seen and always give the "right of weight" to larger powered boats and ships.

Hypothermia

Coastal Vancouver Island is often cool, wet and windy and sea kayaking is often about keeping warm, dry and wind proof. Hypothermia is a progressive physiological condition where the body's core temperature falls below normal because heat loss is greater than heat production. A hypothermic individual will experience impaired physical and mental functions. Most often, hypothermia results from a sequence of events: a cold night in a damp sleeping bag, a poor breakfast, a long tiring day paddling and an unexpected swim in cold water. On cold wet days, wind proof clothing is key to avoiding hypothermia. Fortunately modern clothing options provide a wealth of good choices for paddling and for camping.

To prevent hypothermia always prepare yourself for the worst cold and wet scenario however unlikely that might be. You can be proactive in preventing heat loss by having sufficient food, water, and and protective clothing to keep the heat in, and by staying active enough to generate sufficient body heat.

Food and Water

Food and water are necessary to keep you warm and give you the energy to keep the kayak moving forward. Clean drinking water is of paramount importance. Many products are available to filter or purify drinking water. All groundwater collected for drinking should be filtered and treated. Remember that your water is only as clean as your filter, your containers and your hands. It is one thing to accept some sand in your salsa but lack of personal hygiene and careless food preparation can result in sudden and debilitating illness.

Fishing and shellfish harvesting

Fishing licenses are required for any fishing or collecting of shellfish. The waters around Vancouver Island are renowned for salmon, halibut and ther sports fish. Regulations based on conserving fish stocks means that there are fishing restrictions on some areas during specific seasons, and there are also limits according to species, body size and number of fish caught or shellfish collected.

The shoreline can yeild and abundance of shellfish, both edible and non-edible. Before you leave home, contact fisheries or local health officials and ask about red tide paralytic shellfish poisoning (PSP) and other Harmful Algal Blooms (HAB's) in the area where you will be travelling. If the area is clear, you can dine on clams, mussels, and oysters. Crabs, limpets, and abalone are generally less affected, but do not eat any shellfish without accurate, up to date information.

Encounters with animals

Sea kayakers can have a considerable impact on animal populations that have few other intruders. In general the best practice is not to approach any wildlife too closely. The following are examples of what can happen if you get too close:

- Cormorants nesting on cliffs fly off exposing eggs to predators
- Oyster catchers nesting on rocky intertidal areas fly off leaving eggs to chill.
- Sea otter moms dive, dunking pups that were warm and dry resting on mom's chest
- Harbour seals vacate haul-outs where they were resting and nursing young.
- Seal lions vacate haul-outs in a panic, crushing pups.
- Bald eagles cease feeding and depart the area.

In areas where kayaks are very common, repeated interactions with whales cause stress and avoidance of feeding and rest areas.

Federal wildlife regulations require non-interference by humans and a minimum distance of 100 metres from marine mammals.

Cougars, wolves and bears – oh my!

Cougars, wolves and bears are all found on Vancouver Island. Seeing them is usually an exciting and rewarding experience, providing both you and the animal are unharmed. If you do experience a confrontation, immediately inform the nearest Conservation Officer.

When animals come into conflict with humans, the animals quickly lose. It is in the animal's best interest to avoid any close contact, leaving the animals unaccustomed to and wary of humans is the safest for all concerned.

Here are some tips to help you avoid a confrontation:

- Survey potential camping areas for signs of wildlife trails. Animals use an open beaches as walkways, so place your tent away from their morning routes.
- Avoid taking along items that might attract animals such as fresh fruit, meat, fish or perfumed cosmetics. Instead, take canned or freeze-dried goods.
- Keep your campsite very clean at all times. Wash dishes in a container and dispose of grey water at sea.
- Cook and eat well away from your tent.
- Hang your food and food preparation items, including dishcloths, cooking aprons, garbage, toiletries and cosmetics.
- Never feed or approach wildlife. It is an offense to feed or harass wildlife and offenders can be charged (in more ways than one).
- Do not allow animals to approach any closer than 100 metres.
- Always give animals an avenue of escape.
- Hike as a group. Always keep children in sight.
- Sleep in your tent. Most animals will walk around a tent without venturing in.

Cougars

Although cougars inhabit most regions of Vancouver Island they are elusive and rarely seen and not common along beaches. They are most active at dawn and dusk but will roam and hunt at any time of the day or night and in all seasons. Cougars are stealthy predators capable of bringing down large prey.

Tracks Claws are retractable and do not show in tracks.

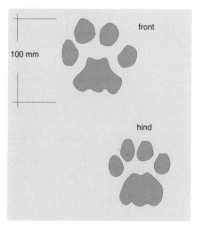

front

100 mm

hind

If a cougar persists or behaves aggressively

- Do not run. Do not turn your back
- Stay calm, remain upright, face the cougar and talk in a confident voice. Do all you can to enlarge your image.
- Arm yourself with a large stick, throw rocks and speak loudly. Convince the cougar that you are a threat, not prey.

Wolves

Wolves use beachs as a transportation corridors and sea kayakers have encountered wolves along the Island's west coast from Cape Scott to Tofino. Wolves will feed on human excrement so toilet areas should be below high tide, well away from camp.

Typically, wolves are secretive and will run away when they encounter people. Never feed a wolf. Feeding wolves leads to them becoming unafraid and aggressive toward people.

If a wolf approaches

- Make noise, look big and dangerous and throw sticks, rocks and sand at the wolf.
- Convince it you are a threat, not prey.

Wolf tracks

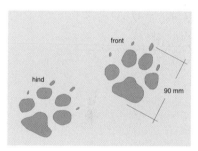

front

hind

90 mm

Bears

Black Bears can be encountered anywhere on Vancouver Island. Bears have keen eyesight, good hearing, an acute sense of smell, and are agile tree climbers. They are strong swimmers and will visit offshore islands. Bears use beaches as a transportation corridors and often feed on small crabs, sand fleas, and maggots found amongst boulders and piles of kelp along the beach. Bears unfamiliar with humans make every effort to avoid contact but a bag of garbage or some unattended food may prove irresistible to their extremely keen sense of smell. Food or garbage left inside a kayak is no deterrent from a bear's continuous search for food. Bears quickly learn to scavenge campsite food losing fear of humans and become a serious threat.

Bear tracks

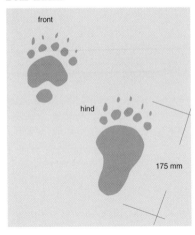

If you see a bear
- Remain calm, keep it in sight, and avoid direct eye contact.
- Make your presence known. This may be difficult on a gravel beach with pounding surf. To avoid surprising any animal you may need to bang cooking pots together or use an air-horn. Upon identifying you, the bear should dash away.

If a bear approaches
- Move away, keeping it in view.
- Avoid direct eye contact. Remain self-assured and protect yourself with sticks and rocks.

Small animals

There is often more damage inflicted on campers by slugs, crows, ravens, mice, raccoons and squirrels than by their larger animal friends. The same rule applies to the small animals as applies to large mammals; keep a clean campsite, don't take food into your tent—and if a slug approaches, avoid direct eye contact.

Venomous creatures

There are no venomous insects on Vancouver Island and its one or two venomous spiders are very rare. According to the BC Ministry of Forests, the venomous brown recluse spider has never been recorded in British Columbia or anywhere else in Canada. However, anecdotal evidence suggests otherwise. Fact or fiction, it is extremely rare. Black widow spiders are known to exist. For both spiders you are at greatest risk when choosing fruit at the supermarket.

There are no venomous snakes on Vancouver Island.

1

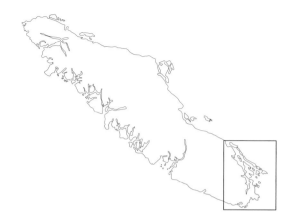

Victoria to Nanaimo & the Gulf Islands

Distance 67 nmi
Duration 5 travelling days
Charts #3440, #3441, #3442, #3442
Tides and Current Tables Vol. 6
> Due to complex hydrography Victoria Harbour tide heights are unique sometimes exhibiting only one high and one low tide per day.
Tide Reference Stations Height for Fulford Harbour on Salt Spring Island provides good general information for the area.
Current Reference Stations Race Rocks, Active Pass, Dodd narrows, Polier Pass, Gabriola Pass. **Secondary stations** Bains Channel, Sidney Channel, Boundary Pass, Boat Pass
Weather Broadcast Regions Straits of Juan de Fuca, Haro Strait and the Strait of Georgia.
Weather Reporting Stations Trial Island, Discovery, Haro Starit, East Point, Ballenas, Sisters Island
Coast Guard Services Victoria, Oak Bay, Brentwood, Browning Hbr., Patricia Bay, Mill Bay, Cowichan Bay, Sidney, Ladysmith.Hbr., Ganges, Nanaimo

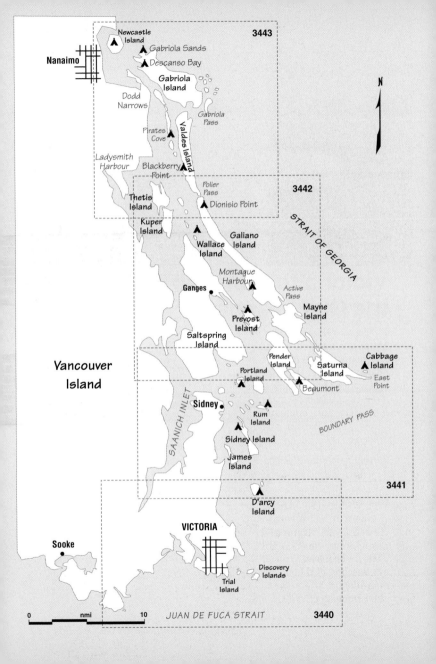

Looking out from Discovery Island to the conjunction of Haro Strait and Juan de Fuca Strait. Mount Baker (Washington State in the distance)

The southwestern shore of Vancouver Island lies in the rain shadow of Washington State's Olympic Mountains creating an unexpected dry environment with less than 1/10 of the average annual rainfall of the west coast. The cool waters of the Pacific provide a moderating influence making for warm winters and cool summers. With low precipitation and mild temperatures, the rocky archipelago of the Gulf Islands has a distinctive local environment.

The Gulf Islands are a dry ecosystem with minimal fire-fighting capacity. Within the region's park system open fires are restricted or not allowed at all. Regional district and municipal by-laws do not allow open fires on beaches.

The landscape of the gentle Mediterranean-like environment is characterized by Douglas Fir, Gary Oak and Arbutus trees. Tidal currents are funneled by the Juan de Fuca Strait and struggle to change direction around the south end of Vancouver Island and are then are further strained through the Gulf Islands. The turbulent current provides a foundation for a rich marine ecosystem. This ecosystem includes breeding habitat for great blue heron, oyster catchers, cormorants, numerous other shorebirds, and waterfowl. The irregular rocky shoreline provides quiet areas for harbour seals to haul-out and give birth. California sea lions and occasionally Stellar's sea lions and a few gargantuan Elephants seals haul out to rest before migrating north. The region is home to resident pods of killer whales that are present throughout most of the year. Grey whales and transient killer whales periodically find they way in from the open Pacific.

In some locations, to cross from Canada to the U.S. can be little more than a 2 mile paddle and kayakers making an international passage must abide by the international regulations for any vessel crossing the border.

Paddling Conditions

The moderate and generally stable weather of southwestern Vancouver Island provides ideal paddling conditions for all levels. Kayak touring is popular six months of the year yet more hardy local paddlers may be out paddling year-round.

As the tide rushes in through the Juan de Fuca Srait the current is constrained and forced to turn 180°. As a consequence, currents can be locally strong and run at 5 or 6 knots in many locations and much faster in a few passes. A thorough understanding of tidal currents and an ability to read tide and current tables is a necessity. In many instances knowledge of local current patterns is very useful. *Current Atlas: Juan de Fuca Strait to Strait of Georgia* may help unlock some of the mystery associated with the complex currents swirling about southern Vancouver Island. (see reference in appendix)

Safety considerations

The velocity of tidal currents increases dramatically at headlands where the geography forces a change in direction. Near Victoria, the waters surrounding Trial Island and Discovery Island can be deceptive and potentially dangerous. Boiling Reef adjacent to East Point on Saturna Island can also have hazardous combinations of current and wind.

In these locations, when the current changes direction to appose an increasing wind, sea conditions can quickly become very difficult. A number of isolated channels have very strong, hazardous currents. Polier Pass, Active Pass, Dodds Narrows and Gabriola Pass can be navigated only near times of slack water. Active Pass should be generally avoided because of the complicating effects of strong currents and very busy ship and ferry traffic. Detailed, up to date current information for each of these passes is available in the tide and current tables. Familiarly with the tables and some good judgement makes paddle these areas popular and safe.

Numerous beaches and small coves are always close at hand for easy landing of a kayak. Where beaches back onto private property courtesy is expected. If you must go ashore at these locations, remain below the limit of high water and do not light any fires.

There is a great deal of marine traffic on these waters. Juan de Fuca Strait, Haro Strait and Boundary Pass are some of the busiest shipping lanes in the world. BC ferries leave and arrive at the terminal at Swartz Bay near Sidney at least once an hour and take routes to Vancouver and a number of the Gulf Islands. These large ships move quickly and have limited maneuverability in the narrow passage of the Gulf Islands. To the north, scheduled ferries also run to Vancouver from Departure Bay and Duke Point near the city of Nanaimo. Tugs and barges are common and must also be avoided. During summer months yacht traffic can be considerable. With all this boating traffic the complex shoreline stills provides ample safe passages for kayaks.

Fog is common but not frequent. However, because of the large volume of boat traffic, the few foggy days in summer and fall can create significant hazards for the kayaker.

There is good radio and cell-phone communications throughout the region, but the Victoria Coast Guard can be difficult to contact from positions north of Discovery Island.

Principle points of access

Southern Vancouver Island is fully accessible to any mode of transportation. Ferries leave from, Swartz Bay, Sidney, to the Gulf Island and Vancouver, There are also Washington state ferries from Sidney to Anacortes Washington, and a private, Blackball Ferry, from Victoria to Port Angeles Washington. All these ferries take cars and will also take kayaks pulled by hand on kayak-trailers.

Victoria International Airport is adjacent to the town of Sidney and a 30-minute drive from downtown Victoria. Seaplanes operate from the harbour in downtown Victoria and from Saanich Inlet adjacent to the airport.

Several BC ferries run to Saltspring, Pender, Mayne, Galiano and Saturna Island. These short ferry routes provide excellent access to the various islands. Kayaks can be transported by car or walked onto the ferry with a hand powered kayak trailer. If you are walking your kayak onto the ferry, first research a suitable location at which to launch your boat.

The Gulf Islands have a wide variety of accommodations and services with cabins or private beachfront camp-sites. I once took a private campsite on Mayne Island and found, to my pleasant surprise, that it included a large Jacuzzi hot tub right on the beach.

Coastal Trip

⌘ Fisgard Lighthouse – mile 0

Fisgard Lighthouse (1859) was the first lighthouse built in BC.

The light at Fisgard was kept revolving on a bath of mercury by falling counterweights. Every three hours, day and night, for the next one hundred years, the keepers would have to raise the 400 pound weights to begin another repetitive cycle. The 500 pounds of mercury that formed the bearing surface for the light was drained and cleaned every few weeks. The highly toxic effects of mercury were not known and the tendency for keepers to "go mad" was credited to isolation, depravation and slave-like working conditions. These conditions were considered an accepted part of the job and keepers no longer able to continue useful service were summarily released from service without compensation. Today the counter weights, the mercury and the keepers are gone; Fisgard was automated in 1928. The residence adjoining the light is now a maritime museum.

⊠ Trial Island – mile 6

Even though you are close to the city streets of Victoria the seas near Trial Island can be unexpectedly hazardous. Be particularly aware of tidal currents running against strong wind. The waters near Trial Island are a popular place for sea kayak training and practice but the strong tidal currents and

Fisgard Lighthouse (1859).

rough sea conditions south and west of the lighthouse have been associated with several sea kayak incidents.

☒☐ Discovery Island Provincial Marine Park – mile 9

This picturesque park occupies the southern portion of Discovery Island (the northern portion of the island is an Indian reserve) and features 12 campsites in an open field. Campfires are not permitted. A hiking trail system runs from the lighthouse on Sea Bird Point to the western shore of the park and along several gravel beaches. Although close to downtown Victoria, the south shore of Discovery Island can be remarkably quiet and seemingly remote.

The adjacent Chatham Island is an Indian reserve and paddling the sheltered waters between Chatham and Discovery Island is a joyful experience. Nearby to the west, between Oak Bay and Discovery Island is the Chain Islets archipelago, an ecological reserve and sensitive seabird nesting area. Visitors are not allowed to land on the Chain Islets.

Strong currents and frequent winds can quickly create hazardous rip tides throughout the area, particularly in Bains Channel where currents run to 5 knots. The automated lighthouse at Sea Bird Point marks the junction of Haro and Juan de Fuca Strait. Strong tide rips occasionally develop offshore. When the wind blows strong and the tide runs fast on the south and east of Discovery Island, kayakers are advised to stay close to shore.

Gulf Islands National Park

The Gulf Islands National Park in the southern Strait of Georgia was established on May 9, 2003. With a total area of approximately 26 square kilometers the park incorporates 29 existing sites and parks on 15 islands and over 30 islets and reefs within an area extending from D'Arcy Island in the south to Gabriola Island in the north. Land may continue to be acquired for the park. In 2004 there has been no change in the operation of the Provincial Parks incorporated into the new national park.

⌂ D'Arcy Island Provincial Marine Park – mile 18

This southernmost Gulf island marks the northeast entrance to the open waters of the Juan de Fuca Strait. The campsites on the southern shore are ideal for kayakers, with one caution. D'Arcy is exposed and during strong southerly winds the seas can be rough.

The trails that criss-cross the dry interior of the island tell a story of the forgotten residents. Although leprosy is generally unknown in North America, there have been sporadic cases in Canada. Around the turn of the 19th century, D'Arcy Island was expropriated by the province and turned into a leper colony. Concrete foundations, marked by a plaque are the last evidence of the six small cabins where the lepers lived.

⌘ James Island – mile 22

James Island lies half a mile offshore of Saanich Peninsula. Over the years the island has boasted the best sandy beaches in the Gulf Islands, the best orchard in BC, a private hunting reserve, a horse racing track and a factory that produced 35 million pounds of explosives during World War II. After 50 years of production the factory was closed down. For decades, the security surrounding the factory kept the wandering public away. In the early 1960s, the employees and their homes were moved off the island and spread out onto Vancouver Island and the neighboring Gulf Islands. Today, James Island still maintains its exclusive reputation: it is privately owned and closed to sightseers.

⌂ Isle de Lis Provincial Marine Park (Rum Island) – mile 24

This island was named for the wild lilies that grow there. There are 6 designated campsites within the park designed to protect the island's fragile vegetation. Easiest landing for kayaks in on the shell tombolo that joins Rum Island to Gooch Island (a private island). There is also a very narrow kayak-sized cove west of Tom point. Close to Tom Point a Canadian Naval destroyer was sunk as an artificial reef and site for recreational diving. A number of buoys mark the location.

Located less than a mile from the US/Canada border, the island was a departure point for rum-running incursions into the U.S.A. during the the prohibition years of the 1920s.

⌘ Sidney – mile 25

Also known as "Sidney-by-the-Sea," this small town provides full service close to the community dock and is a great starting point for kayaking trips to the southern Gulf Islands.

The public beach access on Resthaven Road at Ardwell Road is a popular spot to launch. There is also good launching near Sidney along Lochside Drive just south of the Washington State (Anacortes) ferry dock.

⌂≋ Sidney Island Provincial Marine Park – mile 23

Extensive tidal flats, salt marshes and meadows make up Sidney Spit Provincial Marine Park, located at the north end of Sidney Island. The anchorage on the west side of spit is a very popular spot for yachts. There is a wharf and landing floats for small craft. Ashore there are 24 walk-in campsites within an easy walk of the dock and there is a hand pump for water. From June to September a foot passenger ferry runs 2.5 miles from Sidney to the park.

The passage between Sidney Spit and Dock Island is current swept and can be locally rough.

⌂≋ Princess Margaret Provincial Marine Park (Portland Is.) – mile 28

In 1958 Portland Island was given as a gift to Princess Margaret in commemoration of her visit to Victoria. The princess later returned the island to the province as a park.

The park has three campsite areas: Arbutus Point, Shell Beach opposite Brackman Island and Princess Bay. Water is available from a well located on the trail near the mid-point of the island. Campfires are not permitted. Hiking trails circle and cross the island. Be sure to secure all food from the many raccoons. Neighbouring Brackman Island is an ecological reserve and you should not go ashore.

Close to Arbutus Point a Canadian naval destroyer was sunk as an artificial reef and site for recreational diving. A number of buoys and moorings mark the location.

⌂≋⌂ Ruckle Park – mile 32

Saltspring Island is home to the Gulf Island's biggest provincial campground. Extending from Beaver Point to Yeo Point, Ruckle Park has 78 walk-in campsites located along the edge of the forest and across the open grassy area overlooking Swanson Channel. The park is popular with cyclists who ride the ferry to Saltspring Island. The park features a heritage farm with 15 km of trails. A few small sandy coves and one very nice sandy beach provide spots to land and access to the nearby campsites.

⌂≋ Beaumont Provincial Marine Park – mile 32

This park is a few hundred metres from the restaurant and pub at Bedwell Harbour marine resort on South Pender Island. The campsites are spread out on a midden. If you are truly cold and wet you can rent a cabin at Bedwell Harbour. This is a popular spot that allows you to take a break from your own camp-cooking with a meal at the pub and a hot shower at one of the cabins.

⌧ East Point – mile 38

Boiling Reef in the vicinity of East Point Regional Park on Saturna Island is well named: when the wind blows against the strong current the adjacent waters can literally boil.

I had been paddling all day and was about half way between Pelorus Point and Wallace Point on my way to Beaumont Marine Park on Pender Island. After several miles of simple paddling on a calm and dreary day, I stopped in mid-channel to pause. It was so quiet that I could hear the hissing of fine drizzle as it fell onto the calm ocean surface that reflected the grey overcast sky. I could also hear faint puffing sounds, and looking for the source, I noticed vaporous funnels of mist delicately erupting from the water's surface. I was surrounded by dolphins. After a time I looked down and saw one beneath the kayak, moving silently and effortlessly toward me. His eyes were cast down, not looking where he was going; he was approaching quickly. Two shades of dark grey faintly outlined his back against the dappled reflection of the clouds. A white blaze on the underside wrapped up along the flanks more clearly defining his shape. The horizontal tail beat purposefully and powerfully, propelled his weightless streamline bulk swiftly through the water. I was paralyzed by the certainty that he would collide violently with the kayak. Moments before breaking the surface, a stream of fine bubbles began to escape his tightly pursed blowhole. Collision was imminent.

I would have leapt from the cockpit if I could have moved. He raised his head just before breaking the surface and our gazes met. Two metres apart and we were eyeball to eyeball. Upon seeing me he took a right turn that defied all the laws of earthly physics; in less than a thousandth of a blink he had vanished.

Over the years I have found that if nothing is going on I can usually just stop, look and listen, and something will happen.

☒ Boat Pass – mile 36

En route to Cabbage Island, you may need to navigate Boat Pass. The current in the tiny narrows makes passage either very quick or impossible. At various times in the tidal cycle a 1 metre drop in water level across the narrows, makes Boat Pass a popular spot for sea kayakers to practice and play. Boat Pass is listed as a secondary reference station in the current tables. Read carefully because the direction of the flood current is unexpectedly to the northwest.

◁ Cabbage Island Provincial Marine Park – mile 39

Located off the northwest end of Tumbo Island and near the east end of Saturna Island. There is nice camping on the beach and 6 walk-in campsites. The dead trees in the middle of the island are evidence of salt-water intrusion after high tides on stormy days some years ago.

◁ ≋ Montague Harbour Provincial Marine Park (Galiano Is.) – mile 39

This is a very busy park and yacht anchorage. The park has two campgrounds which include 15 walk-in sites for boaters and cyclists and 25 sites for motorists. There is also a walk-in group campsite overlooking the lagoon. A boat launch and wharf are located at the north end of the park. Potable water taps are located throughout the park. (shut off during

Many of the Gulf Islands, like Portland Island shown here, have picturesque dry open woodland. No open fires allowed.

the off-season). Facilities include, toilets and picnic sites. Full services are available at Sturdies Bay and the nearby marina has a small store and coffee bar with basic supplies.

There are a variety of walking trails along Shell Beach and around Gray Peninsula. The white shell beach at Gray Peninsula was used by First Nations peoples for over 3000 years. This area is a haven for many rare and protected plants and over 130 species of birds.

Montague Harbour is a good location for a family basecamp with a recreational vehicle. Easy and scenic sea kayak routes lead up Trincomali Channel.

⌂ James Bay Provincial Marine Park (Prevost Island) – mile 36

At the northwest end of Prevost Island, James Bay offers shelter and a few cozy undeveloped campsites above a pebble beach. While there may be several yachts in the sheltered anchorage, it is unlikely to be busy onshore.

⌂ ≋ Wallace Island Provincial Marine Park – mile 45

Wallace Island is a popular stopover located in Trincomali Channel between the northern ends of Saltspring Island and Galliano Island.

There are 20 walk-in campsites, 9 sites at Chivers Point and 1 site at Cabin Bay which is accessible only by boat. Both sites are ideal for kayak camping. Nine sites are available in an open field at Conover Cove where there is a dock.

There is a water hand-pump (water must be boiled or treated) located on the trail halfway between Conover and Princess coves.

⌘ Thetis Island & Kuper Island – mile 51

There is a dredged channel between Thetis and Kuper islands. Kuper Island is an Indian Reserve. There is a small marina and pub/restaurant at the west end of the channel on Thetis Island, ideally placed for a well-earned break from camp cookery.

⊠ Porlier Pass – mile 50

Current in Porlier Pass runs to 8 knots and has a good deal of boat traffic. The current running out to the pass affects the sea conditions on both sides of the pass. Navigate Porlier Pass near times of slack water.

⌂≋ Dionisio Provincial Marine Park – mile 51

Accessible only by boat, this park has 30 walk-in campsites in two separate areas. Pit toilets, picnic tables, a water hand pump (boil water). Campfires are not permitted. Special kayak-accessible campsites and a storage rack are situated part way between Coon Bay and the park's south boundary. Walking trails are through the forest and along the shoreline.

⌂ Blackberry Point (Valdes Island) – mile 54

Camping is permitted at Blackberry Point. The BC Marine Trails Association(1998) is responsible for cooperative stewardship of the site. Most of the other landing sites on Valdes are within Indian Reserves.

⌂≋ Pirates Cove Provincial Marine Park – mile 57

On the beach above the anchorage, are 7 campsites with tent pads. Facilities include a sheltered anchorage for boaters, and a two dinghy dock. The south side of the park near Ruxton Pass has a wide beach less used for yacht anchorage. Several middens in the park reveal evidence of First Nations use dating back more than 3,000 years. The largest of these middens lies beneath the present campground. Pirates Cove offers opportunity for viewing a wide variety of wildlife.

⊠ Dodd Narrows – mile 61

Refer to Dodd Narrows reference station in the Tide and Current Tables. Navigate Dodd Narrows near slack water.

⌘ Gabriola Sands Provincial Park – mile 66

Gabriola Island is reached by a 20-minute ferry ride from Nanaimo arriving at Descanso Bay. The park's two sandy beaches form an isthmus that divides Taylor Bay and Pilot Bay. There is no camping available. The limestone formations, called the Malaspina Galleries, are located south of the picnic grounds along the beach at Taylor Bay. Natural erosion has carved these impressive arching sandstone formations 4 metres high and 100 metres long.

⌂◆ Degnen Bay – mile 59

There is access at the government dock to nearby Pirates Cove or Blackberry Point.

The Hawaiian Connection Kanaka

In January 1778 Cook was the first European to land in the Hawaiian Islands and the inevitable recruitment of islanders as crew soon followed. The islanders' abilities in small boats and as swimmers quickly earned them a reputation as worthy crew and brought them to the shores of North America.

It is not well known that in the mid 1850's Hawaiians made up 10% of the non-native population of Vancouver Island. Saltspring Island was home to a large enough settlement of Hawaiian's to maintain a cultural influence that lasted for many decades; remnants of which still remain. By the late 1860's Saltspring Island was home to a few isolated homesteads. On the shores of Fulford Harbour and nearby smaller islands Kanaka's were creating a "Little Hawaii" that reached its peak in the 1890's.

Kanaka (the people) was a Hawaiian term adopted by Europeans. When European trading ships arrived in the Hawaiian Island, some Kanaka signed on as crew and when a crew was short handed, others were forcibly conscripted. After the long ocean voyage to North America, some Kanaka stayed ashore to work for the Hudson's Bay Company while others jumped ship looking for better prospects than offered by the 17th century merchant navy.

Travelling around the Gulf Islands one passes Kanaka Bluff on Portland Island and drives up Kanaka Road on Saltspring. The beautiful farmland on southern Saltspring Island, Coal Island and Portland Island was cleared by first generation Kanaka who laboured to survive and build a lasting home in the area. Carney Point and Kamai Point on Coal Island commemorate two early Kanaka families on the island. The beaches in the area were sites where luaus were held to celebrate the harvest and successes of the year. The sea and the land provided a wide variety of delicacies suited to a feast. Salmon, herring, clams, oysters, berries and wild game in abundance made these luaus luscious, bountiful events. As the feast continued from one day to the next, it would move along from one island to another, sweeping up the entire community into a spirit of celebration.

Paddling the short distances between Saltspring, Portland and Coal islands I move along the once well-travelled routes between Kanaka communities. In the shelter of Russell Island the sun is warm and I can imagine the sound of Hawaiian voices in song and the smells of steaming clams and crab with salmon smoking over an open fire beckoning from the shore.

⚓ ⤢ ◆ **Silva Bay – mile 60**
Silva Bay has access and services
**Descanso Bay Regional Park
– mile 65**
(Formerly the Gabriola Campground)
is located off Taylor Bay Road, a short
distance from the ferry terminal. The
park has 32 camping sites. Two bays
provide good kayak access.

⤢ ≋ ⊡ **Newcastle Island Provincial
Marine Park – mile 67**
This very busy family park is reached
by a 10-minute walk-on ferry ride from
Nanaimo. Remains of shell middens
mark at least two First Nations villages within the park. Park facilities
include 18 walk-in campsites, flush
and pit toilets, hot showers, freswater
taps and a food concession. A concession in the pavilion offers a variety of
meals, snacks, beverages.

Short Excursion

Gulf Islands from Sidney – mile 0
Within a half-day paddle from the
town of Sidney are several parks with
good camping and excellent opportunities for sea kayaking. For paddlers
who prefer to paddle a little and camp
a lot, the Gulf Islands with one or two
days paddling from Sidney are ideal.
The milder climate of southern Vancouver Island and the Sidney area in
particular makes this an ideal destination for short off-season excursions.
Overnight trips to Prevost Island,
Portland Island, and Ruckle Park on
Saltspring Island are easy and very
pleasant. Busy during peak season,
the campsites are lightly occupied
in the shoulder seasons. If venturing
farther out to Cabbage Island or Montague Harbour, a ferry ride can make
the return trip safe, dry and conve-
nient as long as you take some folding
trailer wheels along with you.
A one-way trip from Victoria to Sidney via Discovery, Darcy and Sidney
islands is an excellent beginners trip
with some moderate hazards to plan
for, good opportunity for communications and easy access to shore along
the way.

⌘ **Russell Island Provincial
Marine Park – mile 6**
Russell Island is a day-use park at
the entrance to Fulford Harbour
close to Portland Island (Princess
Margaret Provincial Marine Park).
Once a home for Hawaiian settlers, it
has an interesting history going back
to the times of Captain James Cook.
The name Kanaka Point on Portland
Island comes from the Hawaiian
word for "the people." The Hawaiian
homesteads on Russell, Saltspring,
Portland, and Coal islands were all
within easy paddling distance of each
other. See *Kanaka* by Tom Koppel in
the list of references.

2

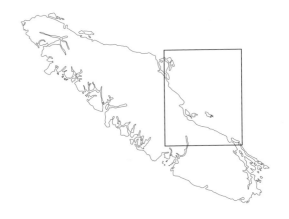

Nanaimo to Campbell River & Jedidiah Island

Distance 80 nmi
Duration 5 travelling days
Charts #3512, #3513, #3539
Tides and Current Tables Vol. 5 and 6
Tide Reference Stations Point Atkinson
Current Reference Stations Dodd Narrows (Vol. 5) , Discovery Passage (Vol. 6)
Weather Broadcast Region Strait of Georgia
Weather Reporting Stations Cape Mudge, Comox, Chrome Island, Sisters
    Island, Ballenas Island, Nanaimo, Entrance Island
Coast Guard Services Nanaimo, Comox, Campbell River, Nanoose, French
Creek, Bowser, Deep Bay

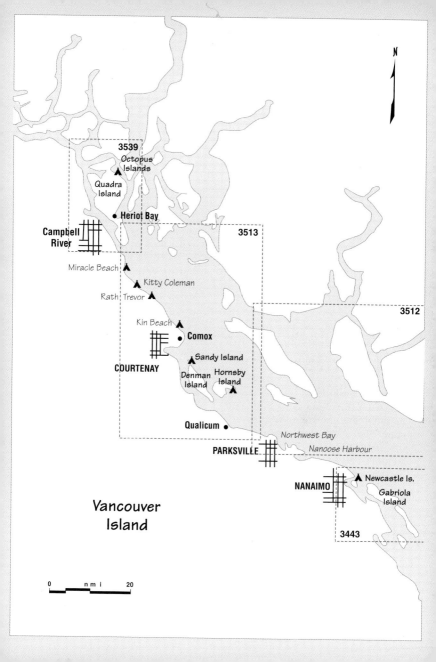

The area's calm conditions, good weather and long beaches make for an attractive holiday destination. Bivouac-camping is hard to come by and the marine parks are busy along what is Vancouver Island's most populated shoreline. You will have to share space with yachts and R.V. campers. In some of the more popular provincial marine campsites reservations are available and are recommended. Seriously consider phoning ahead for a commercial campsite or a B&B along this shore. There is a good chance you can find a private campsite with a pool or hot tub and a nearby restaurant.

Adjacent to Nanoose Bay, the area designated "Whiskey Golf" (WG) is a naval torpedo test-firing range. As ominous as this sounds, the weather radio broadcast announces when the area is active and closed to boat traffic. Travel closely along the Vancouver Island's shore and you will be west of the range.

Paddling conditions

Beginners travelling along shore with frequent landing opportunities will enjoy the warm and calm weather that predominates this region during summer. The region is suitable for beginners taking overnight trips in the company of an intermediate paddler familiar with the area.

Ready access to populated areas and good communications make this an excellent region for intermediate paddlers to undertake multi-day trips. A principle hazard is to be lulled into thinking that the generally good local weather and good sea conditions found near the Vancouver

Island shore are similar a mile or two offshore. A number of kayaking incidents have occurred south of Denman Island and in longer crossings into the Strait of Georgia.

The 8–10 mile open water crossing from Vancouver Island to Jedidiah Island is for advanced paddlers who are very familiar with local conditions and the subtleties of local weather forecasts.

Safety considerations

The region is dry and open fires are not permitted in parks. Dodd narrows and Gabriola Pass are in the vicinity and both have very strong tidal currents with current stations listed in Volume 5 of the tide and current tables.

Large ferries constantly move in and out of Departure Bay and Duke Point so take great caution. A ferry also runs in and out of Buckley Bay to Denman Island.

Locally strong southwesterly winds blow through the valleys of Vancouver Island and into Strait of Georgia. This narrow gap wind, locally known as a 'Qualicum,' extends from Qualicum Beach across the strait to Lasqueti Island. These good-weather winds can build from 30 to 40 knots offshore during the afternoon.

In Baynes Sound at the south end of Denman Island tidal streams run at 2 to 3 knots and can create very rough sea conditions when flowing against a south wind.

Northeast of Lasqueti Island in Sabine Channel, very rough sea conditions occur when northwest or southeast winds blow against tidal currents.

In times of warm weather, northwest winds build starting at Cape Mudge to the north and increase through the day while moving to the south. Forecasts and reports for Sisters Island and Ballenas Island will indicate such conditions.

When tidal streams in the vicinity of Cape Mudge and Discovery Passage encounter southerly winds, dangerous tide rips and overfalls form.

Principle points of access

Near Nanaimo and Campbell River there are numerous points of access along the shore. Parksville and Qualicum Beach also provide ready access to the shoreline.

Coastal trip

⌂≋✗ Newcastle Island Provincial Marine Park – mile 0

Denman Island ferry.

◆ Nanoose Bay – mile 10

The Nanoose Bay military testing range has been operating since 1967. This range, 24 km long by 8 km wide, near shore west and north of Nanoose Bay is designated Whiskey Golf (WG). This range is used to test air-, ship- and submarine-launched torpedoes. No explosives are used; however, a hazard exists due to the possibility of the kayak being struck by the torpedo on its way to the surface. When the range is active, notices are issued on VHF continuous weather broadcasts. Travel by small boats near shore, adjacent to, and west of the Winchelsea Islands and Ballenas Island are not affected.

South Winchelsea Island – mile 10

South Winchelsea Island is owned by The Land Conservancy of BC (TLC). This picturesque little island has an established Garry oak ecosystem, one of the most species-rich ecosystems in

the province. Garry oaks are becoming increasingly rare and in BC occur only on southeastern Vancouver Island, the Gulf Islands, plus two isolated groves east of Vancouver. A conservation covenant restricts camping, fires, pets, non-native plants and seeds and is monitored regularly. There is a rental cottage with accommodation for 6, with proceeds going toward the preservation and maintenance of the island's important ecosystem.

Schooner Cove Marina, located just north of Nanoose Bay has a launch ramp, parking, restaurants, accommodation and other facilities.

⌂ Ballenas Island – mile 14
Near Schooner Cove there are more than a dozen small islands that have small sheltered beaches suitable for camping. You can camp on Ballenas Island and take the shore hike out to the lighthouse.

⌂ Rathtrevor Provincial Park – mile 18
is a popular family camping destination with a large number of campsites well back of an extensive flat sandy beach. At low tide the beach is 500 meters wide. Landing and launching must be done at high tide.

Northwest Bay – mile 16
Northwest Bay offers protection from stormy weather (common in the winter but infrequent in the summer).

≈⌂◆ Buckley Bay – mile 44
is located directly west of Denman Island. It has a ferry service, a restaurant, and a store providing services to highway and ferry traffic. Ferries take 10 minutes from Buckley Bay to Denman Island and 10 minutes from Denman to Hornby Island

⌂◆ Denman Island – mile 40
the island has lovely hikes, beaches and popular B&Bs, but few opportunities for random beachside camping. It is best to arrange camping sites before taking the ferry or paddling over to the island.

⌘⌂ Boyle Point Provincial Park – mile 38
is located on the southern point of Denman Island. It is a day-use park with no camping. If your legs need a stretch you can walk the 1.6 km trail across the tip of the island.

⌂⌂ Fillongley Provincial Park – mile 43
Located on the eastern shore of the island this park offers 10 vehicle-accessible beachside campsites. The park is small and reservations are accepted for some of the sites. Established campsites must be used, random camping is not permitted.

⌂ Sandy Island Park – mile 50
is a cluster of tiny wooded islands located off the northern tip of Denman Island. Random camping is allowed, and there are 8 established campsites in the shelter of a stand of douglas fir near the centre of the island. The park is a sensitive ecosystem: minimize any damage to the groundcover and respect the plants and animals. Open fires are prohibited. At a low tide of 8 feet or less it is possible to walk from Longbeak Point on Denman Island to Sandy Island.

⚓◆ Hornby Island – mile 42

Once you arrive on Denman Island, drive 13 km to Gravelly Bay where another ferry will take you to Hornby Island. Check the overlapping ferry schedules for Denman and Hornby to make certain that you can get to where you want to go at the time you want to be there.

In a northern temperate latitude, Hornby Island is the next best thing to a tropical paradise. Some of the other Gulf Islands make similar boasts, but Hornby's beaches and warmer water seems to be just one step closer to perfection. Warm protected waters and shelter from east and west create Hornby's local climate. Some of Hornby Island past is truly tropical. The rocks are part of Wrangellia, a tectonic plate that started south of the equator and has travelled north for the past three hundred and fifty million years.

⌘⚓ Tribune Bay Provincial Park

Located on Hornby Island, Tribune Bay Provincial Park is known for its beautiful white sandy beach and unusual rocky shoreline formations. Tribune Bay is one of the warmest swimming sports you will find in the Gulf Islands, but you won't be alone there. A village with services and eclectic shops is a 5-minute walk from the park. There is no camping in the park itself, but nearby you will find Tribune Bay Campsite, a large and busy R.V. park and campground. Hornby Island resort is located near the ferry landing offering campsites, rooms and cabins. Rreservations at both locations are strongly advised.

⌘ Helliwell Provincial Park – mile 43

is located on St. John Point on Hornby Island at the northern entrance to Tribune Bay. Here you will find old-growth Douglas fir stands and Garry oaks and other flora indicative of the region's dry climate. No camping is permitted in the park.

⌂≈⚓ Kin Beach Provincial Park – mile 59

This park is located near a residential section of Comox and close to an air force base. There are 18 vehicle-accessible campsites above the rocky beach. Facilities include, pit toilets, fire pits, a woodstove, coldwater taps and a tennis court. A small store selling snacks and toiletries is located next to the parking lot in the day-use area. Random camping is not permitted

⌘ Seal Bay Regional Nature Park – mile 61

The park is a BC Wildlife Watch viewing site where in spring California and Stellar sea lions, seals and migratory birds arrive as they follow the annual herring and eulachon migration. (Eulachon are small, sardine-sized fish.)

⌂⚓ Kitty Coleman Provincial Park – mile 63

Park facilities include a freshwater hand pump, picnic area and 65 vehicle-accessible campsites. Two paved boat ramps and the opportunity for ocean-front camping attract a large number of sport fishers to this busy park. The park includes 900 meters of shoreline and a mature forest estimated to be more than 500 years old.

Cape Mudge, Quadra Island. This day Discovery Passage is clear. It is often current swept and busy with marine traffic.

⌂♨ **Saratoga Beach – mile 68**
Saratoga beach and other private RV parks and campgrounds along this section of coast offer campsites closer to the beach than the provincial parks. Reservations are strongly recommended in the holiday season.

⌂≈♨ **Miracle Beach Provincial Park – mile 69**
Like Rathtrevor Provincial Park this beach is flat, sandy, wide and very popular with family R.V. campers. Campsites are located well behind the beach.

⌂≈♨◆ **Campbell River mile – 80**
is a major regional centre. The southern approaches to Campbell River are host to numerous motels and R.V. campgrounds away from the beach and across the highway. Several boat ramps are very busy with sport fishers

looking for large salmon around Cape Mudge at the south end of Quadra Island. The waters south of Cape Mudge are subject to strong currents and dangerous sea conditions. South flowing tidal currents interact with southerly wind to create steep and chaotic seas.

Short Excursions

Jedidiah Island
The coastline from Nanaimo to Campbell River is primarily long and straight, without any narrow inlets, or archipelagos of small islands. Beyond the quiet beauty of Denman and Hornby islands, Lasqueti and Jedidiah islands beckon to be explored.

⌂✗♨ **Jedidiah Island Marine Park**
is located 10 miles east of Vancouver Island in Sabine Channel between Lasqueti and Texada Islands. One of

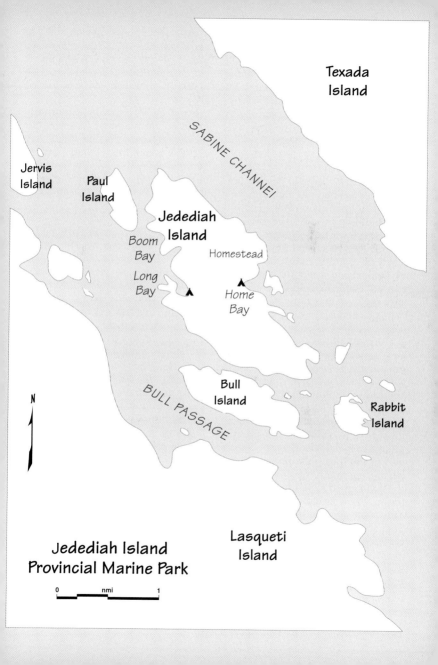

Texada
Island

SABINE CHANNEL

Jervis
Island

Paul
Island

Jedediah
Island

Boom
Bay

Homestead

Long
Bay

Home
Bay

N

Bull
Island

BULL PASSAGE

Rabbit
Island

Lasqueti
Island

Jedediah Island
Provincial Marine Park

0   nmi   1

the largest island parks in the province, it is nestled near to Lasqueti and a chain of more than 30 small islands and rocky islets. Its out of the way location makes it an excellent destination for kayaking and wilderness camping. Random camping is allowed with some of the best sites near Long Bay and Home Bay and small, more secluded sites on the east coast of the island.

The island was sold to the provincial government as a marine park for a little over $4 million. The old farm buildings are still standing, but are now closed and shuttered. Walk around the island and you will see much of the old homestead. Flocks of feral sheep keep the meadows mowed. Unfortunately, farm animals have polluted the groundwater.

Access to the park is by kayak from nearby Lasqueti Island.

The most adventuresome kayakers have paddled from Vancouver Island to Lasqueti. However, this long open water route is prone to strong winds and bad sea conditions that often developing in the latter part of the day. This area has seen a number of kayaking incidents, and it is best to take the private Lasqueti Island ferry which is part of the local culture serving the island community.

The Lasqueti Island ferry, the Centurion VII, is for foot passengers only. The ferry, which departs from the French Creek Wharf on Hwy 19 north of Parksville, takes an hour and carries about 50 people, plus kayaks, bicycles, dogs, and light freight to False Bay at the north end of Lasqueti Island.

It costs about $6 per person and $10 per kayak one-way. To get a boarding pass, arrive at French Creek an hour before departure time and arrange to have your kayak and gear loaded aboard.

From False Bay you can paddle north or south around Lasqueti and take advantage of the tide. Either way Jedidiah Island Marine Park is about 10 miles away through channels and past secluded beaches. The southwest shoreline is rocky and exposed to westerly winds.

Squitty Bay Provincial Park is just north of Young Point near the southeast tip of Lasqueti Island. The park has picnic tables, pit toilets and a public dock. The bay provides shelter from the southerly winds that can blow hard up Strait of Georgia. Camping is not permitted.

⌂ Sabine Channel Marine Park

Includes Jervis and Bunny Islands located in the Sabine Channel. Relatively easy access and a natural protected setting make the park a popular destination for kayakers. The area is pretty enough to attract a steady parade of cruise ships travelling up Sabine Channel.

3

Campbell River to Port McNeill & Cortes Island

Distance 93 nmi
Duration 6 travelling days
Charts #3539, #3543, #3544, #3545, #3546
Tides and Current Tables Vol. 6
Tide Reference Stations Campbell River, Alert Bay
Current Reference Stations Johnstone Strait – Central, Weynton Passage.
    Secondary stations Beazley Passage (Surge Narrows), Okisollo
    Channel (upper rapids), Hole in the Wall
Weather Broadcast Region Johnstone Strait
Weather Reporting Stations Campbell River, Cape Mudge,
Chatham Point, Helmcken Island, Alert Bay, Pultenay Point, Port Hardy
Coast Guard Services Campbell River, Cortes Bay, Port Mcneill

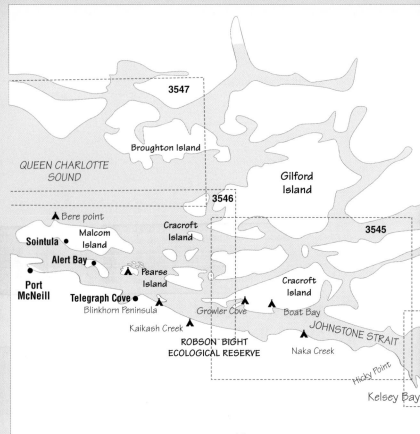

QUEEN CHARLOTTE
SOUND

3547

Broughton Island

Gilford
Island

3546

Bere point

Sointula

Malcom
Island

Alert Bay

Cracroft
Island

3545

Port
McNeill

Pearse
Island

Cracroft
Island

Telegraph Cove

Blinkhorn Peninsula

Growler Cove

Boat Bay

JOHNSTONE STRAIT

Kaikash Creek

ROBSON BIGHT
ECOLOGICAL RESERVE

Naka Creek

Hicky Point

Kelsey Bay

Vancouver
Island

0   nmi   10

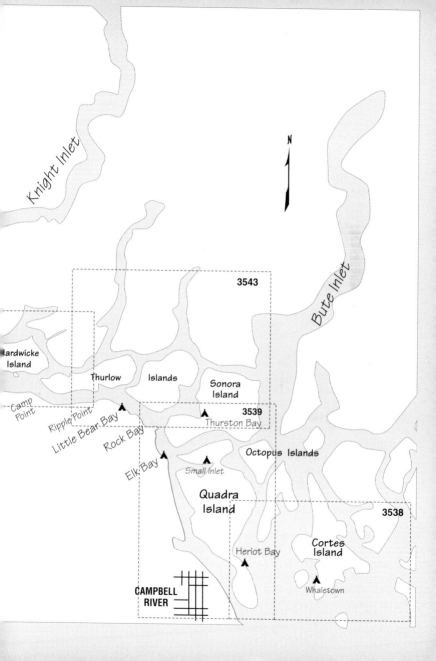

Located between the BC mainland and the northeastern end of Vancouver Island, Johnson Strait is considered to be one of the finest place in the world to view killer whales. From June to October pods of resident and transient killer whales feed and socialize in the area. The complexity and diversity of the marine environment in this region makes for adventuresome and rewarding paddling.

The region is home to the Kwakwaka'wakw First Nation, caretakers of the oldest-known archaeological site in B.C. The village of Alert Bay on Cormorant Island is a centre for native culture and art. The U'Mista Cultural Centre in Alert Bay was established to ensure the survival of all aspects of the cultural heritage of the Kwakwaka'wakw First Nations. The centre contains a culturally significant collection of potlatch and mask artifacts. During summer there are scheduled presentations of native art, dance and other cultural activities.

The Coast Mountains of Vancouver Island descend directly to the shore along Johnstone Strait. Highway 19 is the only paved road in the area. Though this may seem inconvenient, the lack of road access has preserved the region's remote character. In some places, the mainland of BC is less than a mile away but no roads run through the steep, rugged terrain that is deeply furrowed by precipitous inlets. Grizzly bears are not found on Vancouver Island but they do roam the shores of mainland coastal inlets.

Most transportation in this area is by boat. Small logging and fishing outposts were once sprinkled through out the many islands and passages, but such small-scale resource based enterprises have been overwhelmed by increased industrialization in urban centres. The tidal current floods into Queen Charlotte Sound from the north and enters the Strait of Georgia from the south. The tidal streams meet in the vicinity of southern Cortes Island. Although the currents are benign in the region of Desolation Sound, to the east near Quadre Island the narrow channels are extreme.

Paddling Conditions

Beginners frequently arrive in the region of Johnstone Strait for a whale watching adventure. A trip with a certified sea kayak guide is a great way to stay safe in this environment.

Intermediate and advanced paddlers familiar with the area can cross Johnstone Strait in good weather. Intermediate paddlers in the company of a guide or an advanced paddler familiar with the area can make overnight trips. Familiarity with paddling in strong tidal currents is necessary before navigating the recommended passages adjacent to Quadra Island.

All paddlers must remain watchful of the interactions of changing wind and tide conditions.

Safety Considerations

Oceanic weather systems approaching the regions are funneled through narrow passages that open into the Strait of Georgia to the south and Queen Charlotte Sound to the north. Mainland inlets concentrate and direct continental weather systems seaward. Slight changes in wind direction or the passing of a frontal

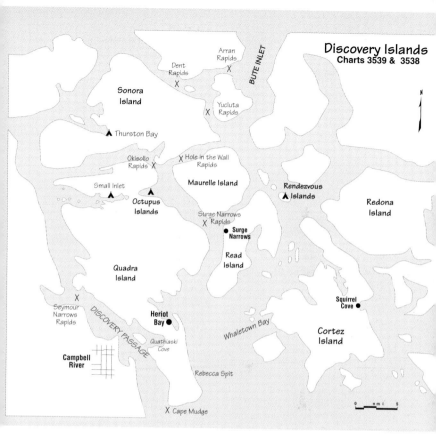

Discovery Islands
Charts 3539 & 3538

Arran Rapids
Dent Rapids
BUTE INLET
Sonora Island
Yucluta Rapids
Thurston Bay
Okisollo Rapids
Hole in the Wall Rapids
Maurelle Island
Rendezvous Islands
Redona Island
Small Inlet
Octupus Islands
Surge Narrows Rapids
Surge Narrows
Read Island
Quadra Island
Squirrel Cove
Seymour Narrows Rapids
DISCOVERY PASSAGE
Heriot Bay
Whaletown Bay
Cortez Island
Quathiaski Cove
Campbell River
Rebecca Spit
Cape Mudge

N

0   nmi   5

weather system can lead to sudden and dramatic changes in local weather and wind conditions. Close attention must be paid to weather reports and forecasts throughout the day. It is of prime importance to have at hand the local knowledge to interpret how sea conditions are affected by weather and tide.

Some channels are extremely hazardous and are not suitable for kayaking. Seymour Narrows and the alternate passages around Quadra Island and north of Sonora Island have violent tide rips, overfalls and large whirlpools covering large areas, making those passages extremely hazardous.

Radio communications in the region are hampered by narrow passages with steep mountains that rise from the water's edge.

Marine traffic

Discovery Passage to Seymour Narrows and through Johnstone Strait is a busy shipping lane with very large ocean cruise liners and freighters passing through daily. Shipping lanes can only be crossed in times of good visibility. There is also considerable commercial fishing, tug, barge and yacht traffic through the main channels and the innumerable passages between the islands.

Principle points of access

In this region the mountains of eastern Vancouver Island climb directly out of the water. Highway 19 follows the shore providing good but intermittent access. There is easy beach access from the highway south of Campbell River. A number of motels and R.V. parks can be found along the beach. A ferry makes the 10-minute run across Discovery Channel from Campbell River to Quadra Island (Quathiaski cove). It is a short yet worthwhile trip. You can launch from Heriot Bay for points to the north and west. There is R.V. camping and a pub adjacent to the ferry dock. There is also We Wai Kai campground a couple of miles to the south in Drew Harbour next to Rebecca Spit Marine Park.

Distances by road from Campbell River

Rock Bay Provincial Marine Park can be accessed via Rock Bay Road (a gravel logging road) 40 km northwest of Campbell River on Highway 19.

For Sayward village (pop 400) and Kelsey Bay, turn off the highway 71 km north of Campbell River. Sayward is a small rural community 11 km down the road. Kelsey Bay Harbour is located 1.6 km from the community of Sayward and is the only small craft harbour located between Campbell River and Port McNeill on Johnstone Strait. A boat launch ramp is located at the end of the parking lot.

Turn off at 188 km north for Telegraph Cove (pop. 20) which is 11 km off the Island Highway via Beaver Cove Road. There is a boat launch and marina and private campground. This is a popular spot for kayak trip departures into Johnstone Strait.

The turn-off for Port McNeill (pop. 2000) is 198 km north of Campbell River. There are accommodations, full facilities and water taxis services.

Coastal trip

⊠ **Crossing Discovery Passage to Cape Mudge**

Discovery Passage between Campbell River and Quadra Island is subject to strong tidal current and a great deal of boat traffic, both commercial and recreational. It is certainly passable in a kayak but not reccommended. Consider taking the Ferry to Quadra Island and starting your trip from Heriot Bay.

⊡ ⚏ ↗ ◆ **Heriot Bay – mile 0**

Heriot Bay is a 10-minute drive from the ferry termonal on Quadra Island. You can find groceries, accommodation and other services en route between the ferry dock and Heriot Bay. There is a pub and a commercial R.V. campground near the public boat ramp. There is also a private campground a couple of miles south down the road towards Rebecca Spit.

On a fine, calm day looking north toward Okisollo Rapids. Hole in the Wall is ahead to the right.

⌘ Rebecca Spit – mile 1

Rebecca Spit Marine Provincial Park has extensive day-use facilities including a playing field, picnic sites, drinking water, pit toilets, swimming, fishing, hiking trails and a boat launch. We Wai Kai Campground is located at the entrance to the park.

From Heriot Bay paddle northeast up Hoskyn Channel. The channel is often breezy, but accept the fact that anywhere in this region, no matter which way the wind blows, it will follow the direction of the channel you are travelling.

⊠⌂ Surge Narrows Provincial Park – mile 9

encompasses the shores of Surge Narrows off Maurelle and Quadra islands and Peck Island in the Settlers Group.

Tidal current charts in the narrows can flow up to 12 knots (see current tables for Beazley Passage). During slack water a route can be paddled close along the western shore of Peck Island and through the left side of Surge Narrows along the Quadra Island shore. Random wilderness camping is permitted.There are no facilities. **Note:** the flood current runs southeast through Surge Narrows out of Okisollo Channel, not as you might expect.

⌂ Octopus Islands – mile 13

Located between Quadra Island and Maurelle Island in Okisollo Channel at the entrance to Waiatt Bay, the Octopus Islands are nestled in the shelter of Waiatt Bay. At night you can lie in your sleeping bag and listen to the sound of the rushing tide at Hole

Killer Whales

The largest of the dolphins, killer whales (orca) inhabit all the oceans of the world, with about 500 populating the waters of British Columbia. For the whales that inhabit the waters surrounding Vancouver Island, a photo catalogue of over 300 whales has enabled researches to identify individuals and their membership in family pods. are intelligent predators with no natural enemies. An adult male can grow to a length of 9 metres and weigh 10,000 kilograms, females are somewhat smaller. Adult males can be identified by their tall triangular dorsal fin, the female dorsal fin is shorter and more curved.

Within the waters of British Columbia, killer whales can be distinctly divided into resident and transient populations. Resident whales live year round in specific areas along the coast. In pods of up to 50 family members, they travel predictable routes in search of fish to feed on. There are two communities of resident whales in the area. The southern group lives in the vicinity of southern Vancouver Island and western Washington State. The northern group of resident whales can be found from central Vancouver Island to the Alaska panhandle. In Johnstone Strait, resident whales regularly visit smooth gravel beaches where they swim back and forth rubbing their backs on the stones. Research suggests, it 'feels good!'

Transient orcas live in small pods of one to five individuals and travel over a larger, less distinct area and feed primarily on marine mammals such as seals, sea lions and porpoises. True to their common name, killer whales will attack and feed on other whales.

To navigate and communicate, killer whales make a variety of clicks and siren-like sounds. Each pod has a unique dialect and researchers can identify family members by listening to these sounds. At times resident and transient pods will mingle in superpods of up to 100 whales.

in the Wall 1.5 miles to the north. Octopus Islands is a popular stopping point for recreational boaters. Random wilderness camping is allowed. No facilities are provided

A 1.5 km portage trail leads to Small Inlet Provincial Park on the west side of Quadra Island; here another trail leads to Newton Lake.

⊠ Hole in the Wall – mile 14

Is a narrow passage leading out of Okisollo Channel between Sonora and Maurelle islands. Tidal streams run up to 12 knots at the west entrance with slack water lasting about 4 minutes. At the east entrance the tide runs at only 2 knots leading out to Calm Channel. Notice that the flood current runs northeast out of Okisollo Channel, not as you might expect.

⊡ Rendezvous Island South Provincial Marine Park – mile 19

is a rocky outpost with a mostly steep rocky shoreline located in Calm Channel off the northeast end of Read Island. The Rendezvous Island group includes: North Rendezvous Island, Middle Rendezvous Island, and Rendezvous Island South. North Rendezvous Island has private lodges catering to sport fishers. The park has no developed facilities; random camping is permitted.

The Rendezvous Islands are accessible via Hoskyn Channel through the Whiterock Passage with tidal stream less than 2 knots. Alternate access can be obtained via Sutil Channel along the eastern shore of Read Island. This route also accesses the Penn Islands.

Calm Channels lead north to the Yuculta Rapids and Dent Rapids with an infamous whirlpool named Devils Hole. This route is long and treacherous and not at all advised.

"Hydrographer Stan Huggett recalls the unnerving feeling of being able to look down 4 metres into the hole formed by one of these whirlpools as his survey launch struggled away from it's edge." *Oceanography of the BC Coast, page 65.*

⊠ Okisollo Channel (Upper Rapids) – mile 16

The Upper Rapids at Cooper Point are reached by travelling north from Octopus Island. Currents run to 9 knots with strong eddies and dangerous overfalls in the vicinity of Cooper Point. Travelling along the shore of Quadra Island there is considerable shelter from the current until close to Cooper Point. A small kayak-sized cove and sloping rocky shore provide a place to haul-out and wait for the current to diminish. **Note:** if you are approaching Cooper Point from the northwest and travelling close to shore you will not see around the corner until you are very close to a nasty big wave at the point. Flood current runs north to south.

⊠ Okisollo Channel (Lower Rapids) – mile 17

There is another obstacle a mile farther along, the Lower Rapids. The preferred route is to avoid the very turbulent waters over Gypsy Shoals and cross Okisollo Channel north to Barnes Bay.

Campsite in Okisollo Channel near Octopus Islands.

⌂ Small Inlet Provincial Marine Park – mile 27

Located in Kanish Bay on the northeastern shore of Quadra Island. From the southeast corner of Small Inlet there is a rough 1.5 km trail leading to Newton Lake. Another 0.8 km trail makes a portage possible from the park across to Waiatt Bay in Octopus Islands Provincial Marine Park. There are no developed facilities and random camping is permitted.

⌂ Thurston Island Provincial Marine Park – mile 31

This park has two parts: Thurston Bay on the northwest side of Sonora Island and along the north side of Burgess Passage leading to Cameleon Harbour. There is a secluded lagoon at the south end of Thurston Bay and there are small beaches nestled along the rocky shoreline. The park has no developed facilities and random camping is permitted.

For a great view of the area walk the rough trail from the park up Mount Tucker (elevation 836 m). Another trail leads to Florence Lake for swimming and nearby there are numerous small coves and beaches.

Johnstone Strait

When departing Okisollo Channel cross Discovery Passage and remain on the Vancouver Island shore. Avoid crossing Southern Johnstone Strait. The strait is a wind tunnel and with a turn of the tide against the wind, sea conditions in the middle of the strait can be rough to very dangerous.

Blown Ashore Landing

The tide is full, the wind is calm, it is the middle of the night and the rising full moon casts enough light to draw long shadows on the ground. I sat up late and watched the night sky until finally I found my way into the sleeping bag.

I overslept and when I awoke some of the best hours for paddling had past. A half breakfast is gobbled while I pack up. The mid-day breeze has begun to rise and departing the shore it pushes on my back urging me eastward down and across Johnstone Strait

Throughout the day the waves grow with the rising wind, and a contrary tide pushes the crests close together. Some one-and-a-half meter waves are breaking steep enough to allow an occasionally good surf ride. In an attempt to shorten the crossing and avoid any heavier weather I try to alter course westward toward the shore, still over a mile away, but the wind and waves propel me down the straits.

Paddling downwind, I have been lulled into complacency. The weather has increased and, in a dramatic display of power, the wind increases to a near gale. Until now paddling has been fun, but conditions are rapidly getting out of hand. Surfing a breaking wave past a tiny sheltered cove I turn upwind to make my way in toward shore, but the weather pushes me back and I can't paddle against it. I am forced to turn and continue downwind. The wind continues to increase and the situation is becoming dangerous. Gusts reflect off the shoreline and come at me from the side. I have to lean into the gusts to avoid capsizing.

About half a mile ahead, on the next headland, there is a sandy patch not more than ten meters wide. Determined not to miss this one I turn a little off the wind. The unnavigable tide rips in mid-channel are expanding leaving a decreasingly narrow safe lane near shore. The tiny beach is the last safe haven before being propelled around the headland to the next unknown. When the kayak's bow cuts onto the sand I take my first conscious breath in over an hour. I can breath but I can't relax; it will take some time to untangle the bird nest of knots in my muscles.

I have arrived here as flotsam, cast upon a leeward shore in a gale. Clearly, I let the weather build over a safe limit. The wind on my wet clothes quickly chills me through. I must get dry, make camp and have a hot meal as I missed lunch somewhere in the middle of the strait. In my camp, short dense fir trees provide an almost impenetrable windbreak around a level spot covered with long grass. For the time being I am secure in the grass behind the trees.

With a quick change into dry clothes and a hot meal consumed, my sleeping bag beckons. The wind will calm and the tide will be still in the early morning. It is still broad daylight and before I finish zipping up my sleeping bag my head is down and I am out. There will be no lingering beneath the moon tonight.

⌂⚓ Elk Bay Recreation Site – mile 24

Elk Bay is located on the shore of Vancouver Island, west of Okisollo Channel. There is a small sandy beach and some established campsites on the southern shore. The site is accessible by gravel road. A number of larger vessels stop in Elk Bay prior to moving on through Seymour Narrows.

⚓ Rock Bay Provincial Marine Park – mile 29

Rock Bay Provincial Marine Park straddles Chatham Point on Vancouver Island at the junction of Discovery Passage and Johnstone Strait. The park includes the bays on either side of Chatham Point and is accessible from the ocean and by road. There is a boat launch only and all operations near the park are private.

⌂⚓ Little Bear Bay Recreation Site – mile 30

Little Bear Bay is located 2 miles west of Chatham Point. There you will find a rough boat launch and a campsite area. The site is accessible by a gravel side road off Rock Bay Road.

⊠ Ripple Point – mile 33

The current can run to 5 knots off Ripple Point and a dangerous rip can form.

⊠ Camp Point – mile 43

western approaches to Kelsey Bay through Current Passage and Race Passage are subject to strong current and hazardous tide rips. The route along the Vancouver Island shore is generally out of harms way. A keen awareness of current and wind direction is still strongly advised.

The view from the Octopus Islands looking west across Waiatt Bay to Quadra Island.

⌂ Kelsey Bay – mile 48

In Kelsey Bay Harbour has public docks and a boat launch. You may find some provisions available nearby.

⌧ Hicky Point – mile 54

Is known to be a little windier than other points else nearby including nearby Windy Point. In strong west wind there may be some shelter to be found east of Windy Point in St. Vincent Bight.

⌂ Naka Creek Recreation Site – mile 67

In the site of an old logging camp there is nice beach and room for camping. This site is accessible by logging road.

Telegraph Cove

Nestled in a remote cove on northeastern Vancouver Island, Telegraph Cove was established in 1912 as a lineman's station to support the telegraph line from Campbell River to the north end of the island. Across Broughton Strait on Cormorant Island is the village of Alert Bay. Telegraph Cove is backed by steep mountains densely guarded by towering evergreen forests choked with salal. At the turn of the century Alert was home to a dozen whites and 200 Kwakiutl Indians. On a calm day, passage from Telegraph Cove to Alert was 3 miles, on a stormy day, of which there were too many, there was no way out of Telegraph Cove.

In time, a small saw mill and a salmon saltery were established and produced enough lumber and salt fish for export to the established communities in and around Vancouver. Through the years following the great depression, Telegraph Cove grew slowly and steadily but not without immense effort and sacrifice by the few residents. Without level land to build upon the sawmill, saltery and a few houses were built on pilings rising out of the water. The rain dominated the weather for months and at times the deluge blurred the difference between air and sea. The hazards of working in the forest and on the ocean took their toll. Dreadful injuries were part of life there and communication with the outside world was slow and capricious. The lack of any road out of the cove sometimes contributed to an untimely death.

With the coming of the Second World War the demand for lumber was insatiable and the mill worked at its capacity. For several years the community grew and life ran at a fever pace. The end of the war brought quiet isolation back to the remote cove. Meanwhile the increasing productivity of larger saw mills and modern fish processing plants closer to mass markets started an inexorable decline in the demand for their products. In the middle 1960's the road reached Telegraph Cove and it was never to be the same again. Local residents gained access to the goods and services of towns like Campbell River. The trip to Victoria that was once a two-day boat trip if the weather was good was reduced to several hours by car. The road also brought the tourists.

Telegraph Cove now has a restaurant, a yacht marina and a large parking lot chock-a-block with of RV's and hi-powered sport fishing boats.

⌘ Robson Bight Ecological Reserve (Tsitika River) – mile 73

Although this ecological reserve is closed to the public, the surrounding area provides good opportunities for camping, boating and whale watching.

Robson Bight (Michael Bigg Ecological Reserve) is located in Johnstone Strait 20 km south of Telegraph Cove. It was established in 1982 to protect important killer whale habitat. This area is one of several where whales like to rub themselves against the beach gravel. Wardens patrolling the area off the mouth of the Tsitika River will request visitors to stay clear. The reserve includes the bight and a 1 km offshore buffer zone.

If you cross Johnstone Strait at this point you will access Alert Bay, Sointula and the Broughton Archipelago.

⌂ Boat Bay – mile 73

Whale researcher/observers on Cracroft Island use the island's bluffs as a vantage point to watch whales in Robson Bight. There is camping in Boat Bay, but whale researchers often occupy the best spots.

⌂ Growler Cove – mile 77

There is limited wilderness camping in Growler Cove and out on the point. This sheltered spot is a popular with boaters who stop to watch the whales go by or to do some sport fishing.

Side trip to Mamaliliculla

Growler Cove it is not far from the ancient village of Mamaliliculla, located on Village Island at the mouth of Knights Inlet. The Kwakwaka'wakw people have inhabited this site for centuries.

Village Island and nearby Mound Island are traditional Kwakwaka'wakw sites. Abandoned for many years, the traditional site was overgrown. Since 1996 the collection of landing and camping fees have helped fund the restoration and ongoing maintenance of the village and neighboring campsites. During summer Mound Island hosts ten or more campers each night of which more than half arrive by kayak. There may be someone on site to collect fees or give permission prior to landing. Mound Island is popular with sea kayak tours and charter groups (see phone number at the back of the book)

⌂♨ Kaikash Creek Recreation Site – mile 78

The camping area at Kaikash Creek is likely to be crowded during peak season. Fresh water can be found, but you may have to walk up the creek. A caretakers cabin is to be built on site and fees are scheduled to be put in place which may assist in the clean up and sharing of this busy site.

⌂ Blinkhorn Peninsula Recreation Site – mile 81

Blinkhorn Peninsula was once the site of a logging camp. This is a busy camping area and fees are soon to be charged.

⌂♨⌒◆ Telegraph Cove – mile 83

⌧ Blakney, Blackfish Sound, Pearce Passage(s)

These areas have swift-moving tidal currents and are subject to tide rips that can be hazardous in windy conditions. Refer to tidal current tables for current velocities and directions.

⌂ Cormorant Channel Provincial Park – mile 85

is situated at the western end of Johnstone Strait between Hanson Island and Cormorant Island. The park includes a number of undeveloped islands in the Pearse and Plumper groups. When wind and current conditions permit, make the 2-mile crossing to Pearse Island. Currents in Pearse Passage can run to 4 knots with tide rips. Check the current tables for the time and velocity of current in Johnstone Strait and Weynton Passage before you start.

The area is part of the very popular Johnstone Strait sea kayak destination. There are a number of isolated places to haul-out and camp among the many islands, but anticipate many of them to be occupied.

⌂◆⚓✗◆Port McNeill – mile 93

With a population of 3,000, the town has a long history as a center for logging. The downtown core has a full range of services and accommodations. There is regular ferry service from the harbour to Alert Bay and Sointula. One-way trips take approximately 30 minutes. See Section 4 (short excursions) for details on ferry routes and paddling opportunities near Port McNeill.

There are a number of kayak outfitters offering whale watching and also a water taxis service available.

Short Excursions

Cortez Island

East of Quadra Island, are the popular waters of Desolation Sound. While the area has a feeling of quiet island life and coastal wilderness about it the number of yachts using the area can be quite substantial. The Mediterranean-like climate and warmer water attracts pleasure boats from around the world and the yacht traffic may be the greatest hazard in the area. Cortex Island is located at the convergence of three climatic zones: the sheltered region of the Strait of Georgia to the south, the coastal oceanic region of Queen Charlotte Sound to the north and the fjord-lands of the BC mainland to the east. Both air temperature and water temperature rise considerably at this crossroads. Recreationists experience the dense temperate rain forest clinging to steep mountainside plunging into the water from thousands of metres above. At the southern end of Cortez Island, incoming tidal streams arrive from both north and south creating a tidal doldrum, where the water's rise and fall results in only modest currents. There are however a couple lagoons and restricted harbour entrances that have locally strong currents.

You can ride a ferry to Cortez Island via the 10-minute Quadra Island ferry from Campbell River. A second ferry runs from Heriot Bay on Quadra Island to Whaletown on Cortez. At the front of the ferry line up there is a sign posted to advise you if Smelt Bay Provincial Campground is full. Cortes Island is small with few accommodations and random camping is very limited. Phone ahead early in the season for reservations to Smelt Bay Provincial Park. Stopping there first provides for excellent day trips, the best beach on the island and a base camp to scout out of the rest of this quaint little island.

Don't hesitate to spend a few days in or near Heriot Bay on Quadra Island and paddle day trips from there. Rebecca Spit is a long sandy beach to the south and there are a number of nice coves, bays and small islands along the Quadra Island shore to the north. We Wai Kai campground (open seasonally) is in Drew Harbour and provides good access to the shore of Quadra Island.

Paddling Cortes Island

A large portion of the shoreline is steep and rocky with only a few beach areas suitable for kayak camping. It is best to find a comfortable spot and take day trips. Departing Whaletown and heading north you will soon come to Von Donop Inlet.

⚓ Whaletown Bay – mile 0

The ferry from Heriot Bay arrives in Whaletown Bay. There is a small general store.

⊠ Von Donop Inlet (Ha'thayim Provincial Park)

On the northwestern end of Cortes Island is a undeveloped wilderness park located along a narrow inlet and saltwater lagoon that includes Robertson and Wiley lakes and the surrounding old-growth forest. There are no designated campsites, however random wilderness camping is allowed and down the inlet you may spot some picnic tables on shore. Currents into the inlet are light but at the entrance to the lagoon to the east there is a shallow tidal rapid.

Heading north from Von Donop Inlet the shore is rocky and steep with the fringe of the evergreens reaching down near the water. There are few spots to pull out. Once around Bullock Bluff at the north end of the Island the shore consists of very steep boulders. There is a rocky knoll south west of Joyce Point on West Redonda Island that is just big enough for two small tents.

⌘ Cassell Lake – mile 18

Consider venturing across Lewis Channel and into Teakearne Arm. There is a fun little waterfall cascading out of Cassell Lake directly into the ocean. There is a dinghy dock and a short path up to the lake for good swimming.

⚓◆ Squirrel Cove – mile 20

Lewis Channel runs south into Desolation Sound and the first stop is Squirrel Cove where there is a general store that supplies all the yachts anchored in the cove.

⚓◆ Cortes Bay – mile 25

Cortes Bay shelters dock facilities for the Seattle and Royal Vancouver Yacht Clubs. On the southwest shore there is a public boat launch and parking.

Also see Rendezvous Island South Provincial Marine Park page 57.

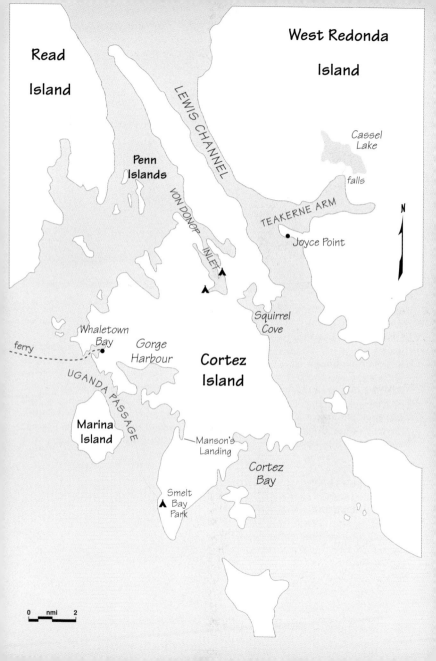

Read
Island

West Redonda
Island

LEWIS CHANNEL

Cassel
Lake

Penn
Islands

falls

VON DONOP

TEAKERNE ARM

INLET

Joyce Point

N

Squirrel
Cove

ferry

Whaletown
Bay

Gorge
Harbour

Cortez
Island

UGANDA PASSAGE

Marina
Island

Manson's
Landing

Cortez
Bay

Smelt
Bay
Park

0   nmi   2

In the shelter of Quadra Island a pair of Bonaparte's gulls with white winter plumage pause to reflect on the days events.

⌂ ᨏ ⚓ Smelt Bay Provincial Park – mile 33

South from Cortes Bay, Sutil Point marks the southern tip of Cortes Island and one of the few accessible beaches. Smelt Bay Provincial Park is a good choice for a base camp and day trips launching from the various spots accessible by the road around the island.

⌘ Manson's Landing Provincial Park – mile 35

The government wharf and picnic area are accessible from outside of the lagoon. The shallow entrance to the lagoon can have swift currents.

⌂ ⚓ ◆ Gorge Harbour – mile 37

has a small general store, restaurant, accommodations and RV park with camping spots. Marina Island lies to the south of Cortez Island and is a flat sandy island with Shark Spit extending out to almost touch Cortez. The current through Uganda Passage may reach 2 or 3 knots during very high tides.

4

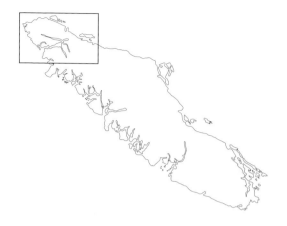

Port McNeill to Cape Scott & Alert Bay/Sointula

Distance 75 nmi
Duration 5 travelling days
Charts #3546, #3548, #3549, #3624
Tides and Current Tables Vol. 6
Tide Reference Station Alert Bay
Current Secondary Stations Nahwitti Bar (on Alert Bay), Scott Channel (on Winter Harbour)
Weather Broadcast Regions Johnstone Strait, Queen Charlotte Sound, West Coast Vancouver island North
Weather Reporting Stations Alert Bay, Pultenay Point, Pine Island, Sartine island, Cape Scott.
Coast Guard Services Alert Bay, Port McNeill, Port Hardy

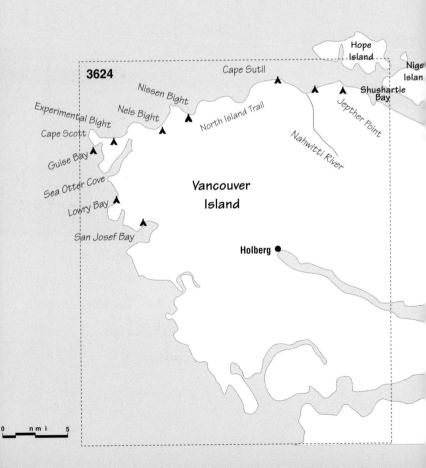

3624

Hope
Island

Nige
Islan

Experimental Bight

Cape Scott

Guise Bay

Sea Otter Cove

Lowry Bay

San Josef Bay

Nels Bight

Nissen Bight

Cape Sutil

North Island Trail

Nahwitti River

Jepther Point

Shushartie
Bay

**Vancouver
Island**

Holberg ●

0   n m i   5

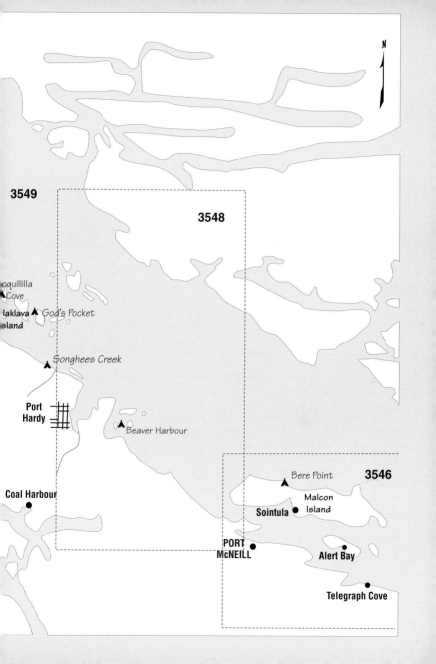

The coastline from Port McNeill to Cape Scott is without major inlets and has only one large protected bay. The coastline changes from the steep shores of Johnstone Strait to the long north-facing beaches at North Island Trail and Cape Scott Park. Once past Hardy Bay there are no roads or villages. The next section of paved road is over 200 miles away in Tofino on the central west coast.

This passage is a grand adventure for the intrepid sea kayaker. Without a doubt you will encounter sea otters, whales, bear and hikers along this rugged and isolated coast. The weather is frequently windy and wet; annual rainfall is between 375 and 500 cm. Even in summer, prolonged sunny periods are a rarity. High winds, rain and generally stormy conditions can be expected at any time of the year. Days with good weather are to be savoured.

This north shore of Vancouver Island is the traditional territory of the Nahwitti people; part of the Kwakwaka'wakw (Kwakiutl) nation. There were once well established native villages in the vicinity of Nahwitti River and Cape Sutil. After many years of productive fur trading the decline of the sea otter led to ill will between natives and Europeans. In 1850, after conflict and the death of several sailors the Governor of the Crown Colony of Vancouver Island, in an excessive show of force, twice ordered colonial war ships to bombard the village at Nahwitti. The village never fully recovered and years later the last inhabitants moved to Hope Island and then to Alert Bay.

In the 1870s the Canadian government opened land for settlement in the vicinity of Cape Scott. A hardy group of Danes made a monumental attempt to establish a community in this extraordinarily difficult place. Unfulfilled government promises and severe weather took its toll and the community dwindled and died.

The shore from Shushartie Bay past Cape Scott is part of Cape Scott Park. The wilderness coast of long white sandy beaches and forests of red cedar, Sitka spruce and hemlock is threaded with many old hiking trails. There is hope to one day build a wilderness trail between Shushartie Bay and Nissen Bight to create a hiking trail that would rival the world famous West Coast Trail.

Paddling Conditions

The route from Port McNeill to Port Hardy is intermediate to advanced conditions. Once past Malcolm Islands the route becomes exposed to the winds of Queen Charlotte Strait. It leaves behind most of confounding effects of Johnstone Strait and is not yet exposed to the open Pacific weather or swell. The sand and gravel shoreline provides numerous opportunities to land without surf. Radio communications between Alert and Port Hardy and among the many boats in the area should be good.

The islands within Beaver Harbour, east of Hardy Bay, are good spots for beginning paddlers in the company of a leader with good local knowledge.

Intermediate paddlers in the company of a competent leader can travel northwest from Hardy Bay through

Flat gravel beach at Port Hardy. The Government dock is off to the right.

Goletas Channel to Shushartie Bay. Goletas Channel has currents of up to 3 knots and can be exposed to strong westerly to northwesterly winds creating very rough seas. Weather and tide conditions are predictable, and there are numerous points along shore to land without surf conditions.

Advanced paddling conditions are found west from Shushartie Bay; all paddlers should have advanced paddling skills and be in the company of a leader with good local knowledge. The north shore is fully exposed to pacific weather and swell conditions. Nahwitti Bar extends across the west entrance to Goletas Channel. Tidal streams across the bar exceed 5 knots, and when an easterly flowing ebb current opposes a westerly wind dangerous breaking seas can extend across

Goletas Channel. While paddling conditions close to the Vancouver Island shore can be much easier, great care must be taken if there is a northwesterly swell creating surf landing conditions on shore. The coastline is remote, with few boats an no roads or communication facilities.

The west coast from Cape Scott to San Josef Bay is potentially the Island's most demanding passage. Exposed to good-weather northwesterly winds and bad-weather southeasterly winds there is no escape from the weather. The shoreline is rugged and although there are a number of beaches, the height and direction of the swell may create difficult surf conditions. Only paddlers with advanced skills and good judgement should make this passage, preferably early in the day during good weather and low swell.

Safety considerations

Once departing Shushartie Bay and heading west, the route is remote and fully exposed to westerly and north-westerly weather and ocean swell.

Nahwitti Bar is notorious for its swift tidal currents and rough sea conditions. Cross the bar only in light winds, low swell conditions and during slack tidal current. A tidal current reference station is listed for Nahwitti Bar.

Cape Sutil, Shuttleworth Bight and Fisherman Bay provide some shelter from westerly swell, but be prepared for surf landings on all north coast beaches.

During times of warm summer weather, northwesterly winds de-velop through the day and can reach to near gale force by late afternoon. Paddling conditions are best early in the day. Winds should diminish through the night making for good paddling conditions the next morn-ing. When the strong northwesterly winds persist throughout the night it can be expected that the wind will be consistent throughout the fol-lowing day and may remain strong for 2 or 3 days before returning to the more usual pattern. Although the weather may be clear and warm it will be best to remain in a well-built camp and wait for the wind to diminish.

The immediate vicinity of Cape Scott is subject to tidal currents that will adversely affect local sea conditions. The passage south from Cape Scott is fully exposed to stormy

Near the Nahwitti River, this bear was sitting down, scratching his belly, watching the kayakers go by.

southeasterly weather and westerly swell conditions. Great care must be taken here; make this passage only in times of fair weather and low swell conditions.

Bears are very common along the north shore so take appropriate precautions.

Principles points of access
Port McNeill and Port Hardy both have easy access to the water and have parking accommodations nearby.

East of Hardy Bay there is easy access to the islands of Beaver Harbour from Storeys Beach.

There is no road access between Port Hardy and Cape Scott. The nearest road access to Cape Scott is at the San Josef River, 10 miles south after rounding the headland at Cape Scott. A return route from Cape Scott requires either paddling a reciprocal route back to Port Hardy or rounding Cape Scott and paddling 10 miles to San Josef Bay.

Refer to Chapter 5 for paddling route information between the San Juan River and Cape Scott.

Coastal trip

⌂⤢◆ Port McNeill – mile 0
Easy launching on the waterfront and parking can be arranged in town. (See section 3)

The shore from Port McNeill to Beaver Cove is rather low and featureless with boulder beaches interrupted with gravel beaches. A few sandy spots allow for easy landings.

⌂ Beaver Harbour – mile 15
This group of small islands and white shell beaches is accessible by road from Port Hardy, and is a favourite spot for local residents. At the head of Beaver Harbour, Story's Beach is flat and sandy, extending well out at low tide.

There is camping on the west side of southern (largest) Cattle Island and on the western extremity of Peel Island.

Deer Island is an Indian reserve; request permission to land or camp.

◆⌂⤢◆ Port Hardy – mile 20
there are full facilities in Port Hardy and easy access to shore along the beach north of town or at the government dock. BC Ferry has routes leading north to Bella Bella and Prince Rupert. The terminal is on the eastern shore of Hardy Bay. There are private campgrounds on the road just south of the ferry terminal, but they are not accessible by kayak.

⌂⤥ Songhees Creek – mile 25
is a pebble beach with easy camping above and fresh water in the creek. Killer whales have been known to rub themselves along these sorts of pebble beaches. The best known example of this is at Robson Bight in Johnstone Strait.

⌂ God's Pocket Provincial Marine Park – mile 29
This park is located on the north side of Goletas Channel at the entrance to Queen Charlotte Strait, and includes Hurst, Bell, Boyle, Crane Islands and several other nearby islets. Pleasure boats travelling along Queen Charlotte Strait seek out the sheltered anchorages found in this park. The park is undeveloped and random camping is allowed.

If you are crossing Goletas Channel, Balaklava Island has good camping across from the Lucan Islands and Loquilla Cove offers a campsite protected from strong westerly winds.

God's Pocket Lodge is located on Hurst Island and provides lodge-based kayaking trips and water taxi service to and from Port Hardy.

⌘≈ Shushartie Bay – mile 38
Shushartie Bay was once a thriving fishing community but is now just one of BC's many small coastal hamlets. There are still signs of the early commercial fishing days. The head of the bay is a large freshwater estuary, teeming with wildlife. The bay offers very limited camping.

⌘ Cape Scott Provincial Park & the North Island Trail
Cape Scott Provincial Park includes over 15,000 ha with over 50 miles of coastline from Shushartie Bay north and west to Cape Scott, and south to San Josef Bay. The area is the traditional home of three First Nations people known collectively as the Nahwitti. There are two Indian reserves within the boundaries of Cape Scott Provincial Park.

An intrepid kayakers dream, this park's shores includes large sandy beaches, small coves and freshwater streams. The park is well known for the wet and rugged hiking trails that lead from the trailhead in San Josef Bay to the magnificent beaches near Cape Scott.

The strip of coast from Shushartie Bay to the Nahwitti River encompasses an old trail that remains undeveloped and not well marked.

Camping is allowed throughout the park. Recent history includes homesteads, farming and raising of cattle on lowland areas behind the beach. The area today may appear pristine wildernessbut you must still boil or treat all drinking water.

⌂ Jepther Point – mile 40
is a steep pebble beach with tent sites up on the shore. The western aspects of the beach can be open to swell and surf conditions. This is the last stop before crossing the waters of Nahwitti Bar, 2.5 miles to the west.

⊠ Nahwitti Bar – mile 42
Nahwitti Bar and Tatnall Reef are tide swept, and west winds blowing against ebb currents can form dangerous tip rips and overfalls. Cross the bar only near slack water and pay particular attention whe a west wind is blowing against an ebb tide. During times of fair weather the seas can be flat and calm with little evidence of potentially hazardous conditions. For times of slack water, refer to the secondary current station on Alert Bay in the tide and current tables.

Tatnall Reef is an extension of a sandy spit and is covered by water 4 to 6 metres deep.

⌂≈ The Nahwitti River estuary – mile 45
East of the river there is a long pebble beach and at the river mouth across from the old cabins there is a flat area for tenting. This area was once a central village for the first nations of the north coast of Vancouver Island.

Intensive logging in the early 1990s has caused significant changes to the mouth of the river and the course of its lower reaches.

⌂ Cape Sutil mile – mile 46

Cape Sutil at the northern most tip of Vancouver Island offers excellent protected camping on east-facing sand and pebble beaches.

The north coast beyond Cape Sutil features four large bays, Shuttleworth Bight, Nissen Bight, Nels Bight and Experiment Bight, each with white sandy beaches interspersed with smaller bays with steeper gravel beaches.

⌂≈ Shuttleworth Bight – mile 50

When the swell and the wind wave are from the northwest Shuttleworth Bight is susceptible to heavy surf conditions. You are more likely to find signs of animal tracks than of hiker's boot on this beach. The Stranby River

course is in good condition with significant stands of timber that have not been logged.

Leaving Shuttleworth Bight the first signs of the historical community of Cape Scott can be found 6 miles to the west in Nissen Bight.

⌂≈ Nissen Bight – mile 57

has nice fine sand and interesting shorelines. Usually there will be a few campers who have made the day-long trek in from the trailhead.

Food lockers have been installed at Nissen Bight, Nels Bight and Guise Bay to safeguard food against bears and other scavengers. It is strongly recommended that you use them.

⌂ Fisherman Bay – mile 58

On the western end of Nissen Bight, Fisherman Bay provides modest protection from northwesterly swell.

The east beach on Cape Sutil is well sheltered from westerly winds.

Cape Scott Settlement

In 1870 the land near Cape Scott was opened for preemption. Advertisements described Cape Scott as lush and unsullied land of promise where 170 acres of meadow and forest were ready for settlement. Fish, fowl and deer were plentiful, and there was opportunity for a new and independent life. In 1894, a small group of Danes accepted the challenge. A few years later a community of 50 was established at the head of Hansen's lagoon. A dyke was built at the head of Hansen's Lagoon to hold back the tide water and reclaim a portion of the meadow. The dyke, 2,300 ft long with 14 ft-high sluice gates was completed in 1899. In celebration of its completion the entire community held a party. The following morning the settlers rose to find the dyke gone, victim to a southeast gale.

Initially the colony hoped to subsist initially on fishing, and with the government's promise to build a road there would soon be access to the outside world. Settlers came from Washington State, the Prairie Provinces, Eastern Canada and Europe and in 1913 the population peaked at over 1,000. The struggling colony survived by fishing and trapping, but after 10 years, the government still had not followed through on its agreement.

Miles of shallow reefs and strong tidal currents make the passage around Cape Scott hazardous in good weather and impossible otherwise. With no natural harbour, Fisherman Bay and San Josef Bay have a history of wrecked ships and lost sailors. Goods that did arrive intact were lightered off ship onto the beach where they were often subject to the rise and fall of the tide before they could be man-handled ashore. Livestock was simply tossed overboard and left to swim ashore. More often than not ships were unable find a safe place to offload and the ship sailed away.

Goods that arrived overland had to be carried along a web of trails that slowly developed between the various cabins built around Cape Scott, San Josef Bay, and Holberg. Many of the trails were even too rugged for pack horses and goods came overland strapped to a back-board. With a standard load of over a hundred pounds, stories of the heaviest loads and the fastest trip became legend. The heaviest loads made it part way before being left behind at the nearest cabin or dropped into a bog never to be seen again.

Without a pier or a road to support a wagon, farm produce could not get out to market. The government's failure to provide a road to the settlement was a crippling blow and the settlement finally succumbed. By 1920 northern Vancouver Island was again desolate. In 1941 the abandoned properties were expropriated. Alfred Spencer, the last man at Cape Scott left his cabin in 1956 when he could no longer carry a heavy load over the trails to his home at the head of the lagoon.

The place names on the chart, Nels Bight, Hansen Lagoon and Frederiksen Point are lasting dedications to the stories of the settlers and the natives who sought solitude and good fortune in this remote place. The artifacts of indigenous and European settlement are evident throughout Cape Scott Provincial Park.

A combination of weather conditions, distance from markets, and lack of suitable access routes spelled the death knell of the settlement. After years of hardship working against the forces of nature and the whims of government, the settlement was abandoned.

Hansen's Lagoon, Cape Scott. Ocean access in the distance in fron of low hill.

To the west, Frederiksen Point is shallow with rock outcrops offshore that can create breaking waves. After rounding the point, Nels Bight appears as yet another long low sandy beach.

⌂≈ Nels Bight – mile 60

This is the most popular camping spot for hikers who have come to explore the inland trails and artifacts of the Cape Scott settlement. There is a park ranger cabin on the west end of the beach. A water hose is located 50 meters to the right of the cabin. At 400 meters long and 200 meters wide, this is the longest of the 9 major beaches in the park. There are a couple of nice camping spots behind the beach out of the wind next to the ranger's cabin. Fifty metres left of the cabin there is a hose bringing water from upstream.

⌂ Experimental Bight – mile 61.5

A rocky headland separates Nels Bight from the Experiment Bight a mile to the west. The eastern end of the beach is not as popular with hikers but provides fine kayak camping.

Farther down the beach at Experimental Bight, past the trail leading to Guise Bay, is the sand neck, an area of sand dunes connecting the north-facing beach at Experimental Bight to the south-facing beach at Guise Bay. The sand neck is remarkably bleak and exposed. There are remains remains of old fencing that once protected the hay field from intruding sand. It is hard to believe that early settlers attempted to grow hay on this desolate piece of land.

Cape Scott – mile 63

The Cape Scott Light Station (1960) is one of the few remaining manned lights on the Island's west coast. You can follow the trail from Experimental Bight to Guise Bay and up to the lighthouse to sign the visitor's book.

⊠ Rounding Cape Scott

Currents in Scott Channel reach 3 knots and can create rough and dangerous seas offshore. In Experimental Bight there is a notable back eddy that can form on an ebb tide (westerly flowing current). When rounding Cape Scott this eddy current can draw you toward the Cape and will dissipate once out of the bay. Near shore, the waters off Cape Scott are rugged and shallow, with numerous rocks and dense beds of kelp.

Although a route close to shore is desirable, incoming swell can break heavily over the shallow rocks; good judgment is needed to select a route though the kelp, the rocks, and the waves. Once around the cape, the deeper, more open waters of Guise Bay should moderate the sea conditions. The first small southwest-facing beach around the point is known locally as Achdem Beach. The eastern part of the beach is an Indian Reserve. After passing Achdem Beach and rounding the small headland you reach Guise Bay.

⊟ Guise Bay – mile 65

Guise Bay faces south and is generally the windiest of the Cape Scott beaches. Prior to leaving the beaches on the north shore, east of Cape Scott you can get a preliminary view of the sea and weather conditions coming in from the south by walking through the sand neck or taking the trail overland to Guise Bay.

⌘ Hansen Lagoon – mile 68

Hansen Lagoon stretches for 3 miles inland. The associated saltwater marsh is a stopover for a vast number of waterfowl travelling the Pacific Flyway.

⊟ Lowrie Bay – mile 70

has good beach camping and a trail that leads overland to Sea Otter Cove.

⌘ Sea Otter Cove – mile 72

The entrance to Sea Otter Cove is strewn with small islands and rock outcroppings. It is fully exposed to stormy weather from the southeast. After threading a course though the rocks and breaking waves, the north shore of San Josef Bay provides for interesting paddling with sea stacks and caves located along the north shore between the beaches.

⊟ San Josef Bay – mile 74

There is often surf breaking across the entrance to the river, and it may be necessary to navigate through low surf to make your way into shore or up the river. There are established camping areas at the first and second beaches on the north shore of the bay. From the most easterly camping area it is a 45-minute walk up the wide flat trail to the parking lot at the Cape Scott trailhead and the gravel road that leads out to Port Hardy. Consequently, this area is often used for day hikes and picnics by residents of Port Hardy and the surrounding north Vancouver Island region.

Camping area at Cape Scott Heritage Park. Boat ramp access in the distance.

⌂ ⌇ ⚓ San Josef River boat launch – mile 75

A boat ramp is located on the San Josef River about 2 miles up river from the beach. The river is tidal and at low tide may reveal shallow gravels bars By land, the boat launch is accessed through San Josef Heritage Park.

Short Excursions

Alert Bay & Sointula

From the heart of the Johnstone Strait whale watching and kayaking area, you can make a wonderful short excursion to the historical native villages of Alert Bay on Cormorant Island and Sointula on Malcolm Island. A ferry from Port McNeill can make the trip entirely day-tripping, or you can use accommodations mixed with camping in private campgrounds.

More adventuresome paddlers can launch from Port McNeill or Telegraph Cove. It is 3 miles from Port McNeill to Sointula, 4 miles between Sointula and Alert Bay and 5 miles from Alert Bay to Telegraph Cove.

Circumnavigating both islands would be a challenging a 35 mile trip with long stretches of beach, interesting European and native history, and some of the best orca whale watching waters in the world. Technical challenges include short passages of swift tidal current and some exposure to the open waters of Queen Charlotte Strait. Frequent good landing sites, readily available local knowledge and good communications make this short trip accessible to a wide variety of skill levels.

BC Ferries operates a regular daily service from Port McNeill to Alert Bay

Tea break on Nels Bight, Cape Scott.

and from Alert Bay to the village of Sointula on Malcolm Island. Each leg of the ferry crossing is approximately 30 minutes.

⌘ ▢ ≈ ⤢ ♎ Alert Bay

Alert Bay village (pop 1000+) on Cormorant Island is the site of a traditional native settlement with a proud heritage. It has many historic sites and contemporary native art displayed on totems and paintings. At 173 feet high, the world's tallest totem pole depicts the figures of some of the tribes of the Kwakwaka'wakw nation.

The village provides a range of services, including restaurants, pharmacy, gift shops, and studios for unique arts and an ATM. The U'Mista Cultural Centre is a showcase of Northwest Coast art and culture

and there are numerous historic sites throughout the village. Accommodations include, inns, B&B's, campgrounds and a hostel. There are laundry and shower services at the government wharf.

⌘ ▢ ≈ ⤢ ♎ Sointula

Sointula (population 800) is located on Malcolm Island. A 25-minute ferry ride from Port McNeill via Alert Bay In 1901 a small group of Finns conceived Sointula as a utopian commune. Early attempts at agriculture were not suited to the island, and subsequent attempts at commercial logging were unsuccessful. By 1905 half of the settlers had departed. The remaining settlers were successful with commercial fishing and ensured the community's survival. Sointula

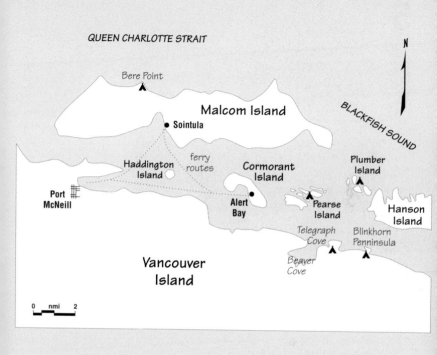

remains a quiet village and Finnish is still spoken.

~

On the island's north shore, Bere Point Campsite in Bere Point Regional Park has beach access campsites with outhouses, firewood, and a boat launch. Other accommodations on the island include B&B's, cottages, guesthouses and a private campground. The 4 km Beautiful Bay Trail through the rainforest leads from Bere Point to Beautiful Bay.

5

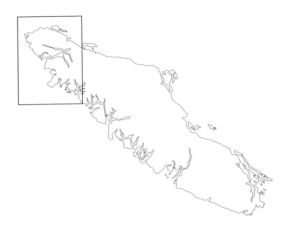

Cape Scott to Kyuquot & Quatsino Sound

Distance 76 nmi
Duration 7 travelling days
Charts #3624, #3623
Tides and Current Tables Vol. 6
Tide Reference Stations Tofino
Current Reference Stations Scott Channel (on Winter harbour)
Weather Broadcast Region West Coast Vancouver Island North
Weather Reporting Stations West Sea Otter, Sartine, East Dellwood,
    Cape Scott, Solander, South Brooks, Nootka
Coast Guard Services Tofino, Port Alice, Kyuquot

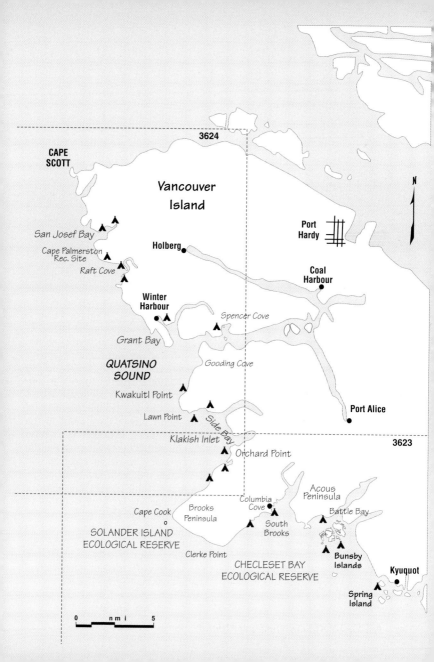

CAPE
SCOTT

Vancouver
Island

3624

Port
Hardy

San Josef Bay

Cape Palmerston
Rec. Site

Raft Cove

Holberg

Coal
Harbour

Winter
Harbour

Spencer Cove

Grant Bay

Gooding Cove

QUATSINO
SOUND

Port Alice

Kwakuitl Point

Lawn Point

Side Bay

Klakish Inlet

Orchard Point

Acous
Peninsula

Battle Bay

Columbia
Cove

Cape Cook

Brooks
Peninsula

SOLANDER ISLAND
ECOLOGICAL RESERVE

South
Brooks

Bunsby
Islands

Clerke Point

CHECLESET BAY
ECOLOGICAL RESERVE

Kyuquot

Spring
Island

N

0   n m i   5

Square-rigged ship at Columbia Cove, Brooks Peninsula..

The northwest coast of Vancouver Island is a region of extremes in all respects. A clear sunny day on one of the mile-long sandy beaches is a sea kayaker's dream, even though the weather lore speaks predominantly of winter hurricane force winds and gigantic freak waves. This section of coast is bracketed by two prominent capes: Cape Scott and Cape Cook. Cape Scott forms the northwestern tip of Vancouver Island and its light marks the southeastern entrance to Queen Charlotte Sound. The famous British explorer Captain James Cook referred to Brooks Peninsula as "the Cape of Storms." Between the capes, Quatsino Sound cuts deeply into Vancouver Island offering refuge from the pacific swell and the full force of frequent incoming weather systems.

The lack of human population is counterpoint to a rich history of native culture. The traditional territories of the Kwakwaka'wakw (Kwagiutl) First Nations extends from the central east coast of Vancouver Island north and west to the vicinity of Cape Scott where they yield to the Nuu-chah-nulth (Nootka) first nation that controlled the west coast. Paddle this stretch of coastline and you will appreciate the seafaring skills of the Nuu-chah-nulth people. The absence of safe harbour kept early European traders offshore waiting for the native to paddle out in their canoes to establish trade.

Today, there is only limited road access along this rugged isolated coast. All the roads are gravel, some are accessible by 2-wheel drive and others are best travelled with the aid of 4-wheel drive vehicles. A passage south from Cape Scott is lonely, wild, and wonderful. There is a good chance that you will see more wildlife than people and you could have more windy rainy days than calm sunny days. Cape Scott to Kyuquot is all about wilderness adventure paddling; it is well worth putting together the necessary plans to traverse this wild coast.

Paddling Conditions

The inner waters of Quatsino Sound are the only part of this region accessible to beginners with a guide.

Intermediate paddlers led by an experienced leader with local knowledge can tour from Kyuquot to the Mission Group Islands, the Bunsby Islands, Acous Peninsula, and southeastern Brooks Peninsula.

Looking from the tent at a rough shore break. Raft Cove beach in the distance.

South from Cape Scott, around Cape Cook and Clerke Point to the southeastern shores Brooks Peninsula, is the realm of the advanced paddler only, preferably with a leader who is familiar with the area.

There is some debate whether this area has the best or the worst paddling around Vancouver Island. Unquestionably, good judgement and seagoing skills are absolutely necessary by all paddlers in the group.

In summer good weather will bring 15-knot northwesterly breezes in the morning and 30-knot northwesterly winds in the afternoon. Summer swell conditions are usually from 1 to 2 metres and can quickly rise higher during stormy southerly weather. Exposed steep and rocky shorelines fronted with shallow water subject to tidal currents make passage around either Cape Scott or Cape Cook a significant challenge.

In warm sunny conditions, the morning will be calm and the afternoon windy. When high clouds are followed by wind backing to any southerly quadrant, you can anticipate a low-pressure weather system with stormy wet conditions.

Safety considerations

The entire region has advanced conditions with significant risks. Travel north to south in stable weather conditions between June and September Mid July to mid August has the driest and most stable weather. Being isolated and without easy communication and rescue services adds greatly to the overall risk in the region. All paddlers must be capable of staying with the group and looking after themselves in dynamic open coastal conditions. Most or all problems will need to be solved without external assistance.

Tidal currents progress northwesterly along Vancouver Island to Cape Scott and accelerate over the shoaling waters through Scott Channel. The currents here are forced to turn eastward and follow the northern coastline. A combination of geography and weather produces one of BC's most treacherous passages. When the outgoing ebb current is opposed by incoming westerly winds, sea conditions can become very hazardous with alarming rapidity.

Shallow waters in the mile-wide passage between Cape Cook and Solander Island aggravate sea conditions. To further complicate this passage, winds at Solander Island are generally 10 to 15 knots stronger than the adjacent reports. To the south, the exposed west face of Brooks Peninsula ends in an extended shallow headland at Clerke Point. Surf conditions that extend well offshore must be navigated before reaching the more sheltered waters south of the peninsula.

Marine traffic

Large ship traffic occasionally moves in and out of Quatsino Sound. Kyuquot is the northern most point of the scheduled service of the *MV Uchuck III* (see section 6). Small boat traffic is rare with the occasional sailing yacht visible offshore.

Principle points of access

There are no paved roads to this section of coast. The area is best accessed along the gravel logging road that leaves Highway 19 just south of Port Hardy. At Holberg, the road branches to San Josef River (Cape Scott Provincial Park) and to Winter Cove. Both areas have camping and a boat ramp. For all other road access along this coast a 4-wheel drive vehicle and familiarity with navigating backwoods logging roads, is strongly recommended.

There is limited parking at the Cape Scott trailhead for the San Josef River boat launch. There is additional parking and camping close by at San Josef Heritage Park adjacent to the Cape Scott Park Boat Launch. For a modest fee, this is a good place to leave vehicles and a great place to create a base camp.

Driving to San Josef Bay

Take highway 19 north. There is a well marked turn-off just prior to the southern limits of Port Hardy. Fill up

Stalking a cougar

Sometimes getting to the launch site is an adventure in itself. In the early morning the sound of a truck moving along the gravel road wakes me up. A voice calls out, "Hey, is anybody in there? If you have any pets or kids stay alert, there is a cougar in the campground."

Sticking my head out of the tent I reply, "No kids or pets in here. Thanks for the news."

The truck rumbles off; once again I am alone. In my tiny one-person tent there is barely enough room for me and a duffel bag, but I will stay alert anyway. Through breakfast I don't see any evidence of the big cat.

Time comes to unpack the truck and load the kayak. The rustic boat launch made of coarse crushed rock is very steep so I leave the truck on top of the ramp and carry my kayak 10 metres to the water's edge and begin emptying the truck and loading the kayak. Ten minutes into to the job, I turn to fetch another armload of gear. There is the cougar sauntering along the road toward my truck. Tawny brown, she is limber and muscular with enormous feet and pert upright ears. The cat, only six or eight meters away hesitates and turns giving me a disinterested glance before sticking her nose into the back of the truck. She turns away, crosses the road and walks into the forest. Up to this point I have been transfixed and unmoving. Her disappearance into the trees sends me into action. I quickly grab my camera and run up the road to cut her off and get a shot as she emerges from the dense forest and into a clearing. Just as I bound over the ditch toward the clearing I have second thoughts, "Should I be stalking a cougar? Probably not!" Coming to my senses I have the unnerving feeling that I am being watched. Walking backwards warily I return my task packing up the kayak. I soon head out to sea seeking safer adventure elsewhere.

with gas and take a good spare tire. After turning west off the highway, the road turns to gravel in about 4 km. The last 63 km are gravel, and you must watch out for logging trucks. Obey all posted signs. Follow the signs 42 km to the tiny hamlet of Holberg. The gas station here may be closed or out of fuel. Continue on the remaining 25 km to the end of the road at the Cape Scott Trailhead. Just prior to the end of the road turn left and follow the narrow road a few hundred metres to Cape Scott Heritage Campground and driving through it. The boat ramp is on the far side.

Logging roads in this area are active with large logging trucks working Monday to Friday until 6:00 pm. It is recommended that you drive active logging roads after 6:00 pm. Be aware though, that there may be logging truck activity at any time and also on weekends. Drive with your lights on and be prepared to yield. Carry at least one good spare tire. For more information on driving the logging roads and current road conditions call Western Forest Product's Holberg office.

Coastal Trip

Departing San Josef Bay the coast is rugged and very exposed for the next 16 miles.

Cape Scott, San Juan River boat launce – mile 0

⌂ Palmerston Creek Recreation Site – mile 6

Half a mile east of Cape Palmerston at Palmerston Creek there is a camp area and tent pads above the beach on the north shore of the creek. This is 26 km via a logging road from Holberg. The road continues along to a parking lot accessible by a rough 45-minute trail to Raft Cove.

⌂ Raft Cove – mile 8

A camping area is located on the south-facing beach less than 1 mile northwest of the river mouth. This end of the beach is accessible from a 2 km long trail that leads from the beach to a logging road. The west-facing river bar at the MacJack River has a significant surf break and a few intrepid surfers find their way to this secret spot. There is an old trapper's cabin a short way up river on the east shore. It is also possible to land and camp at the western extremity of the gravel beach near Commerell Point.

Grant Bay – mile 18

Grant Bay is a beautiful bay with a fine sandy beach on the north side of the entrance to Quatsino Sound. Grant Bay is usually sheltered and less exposed to the open Pacific swell.

Gooding Cove – mile 25

This nice long sand and gravel beach is sheltered from southerly winds and swell. The area is accessible to 4X4 trucks via logging roads. It is not the prettiest spot, but it is sheltered from southeast gales.

⤢◆ Winter Harbour

Winter Harbour (pop 20 - or so) is 76 km from Port Hardy approximately 40 minutes past Holberg and definitely at the end of the road. This tiny remote hamlet is at the tip of northern western Vancouver Island. Winter Harbour was been a safe haven for sailors and fishermen since the 1800's. You may be able to arrange water taxi service from Winter Harbour.

⌂ Kwaksistah Regional Park

Kwaksistah campsite is located at the north end of the Winter Harbour Village not far from the general store. The campsite is a little rough with 12 campsites.

⌂ Kwakiutl–Lawn Point Provincial Park – mile 28

There is easy landing and some opportunity for camping in Restless Bight on the north shore of Kwakiutl Point and on the south shore of Lawn point northwest of Rugged Islands.

Side Bay – mile 34

To the east of Kwakiutl Point, the beach at Side Bay, is usually more sheltered and can be a welcome stop with potential camping spots. There is an Indian Reserve on the west shore of Keith River. A logging road runs behind the shore of Side Bay.

Camping at Brooks Peninsula. We found a Japaneese glass fishing float 5 metres from the tent.

Klaskino Inlet – mile 36

The southern shores of Klaskino Inlet and Klaskino Anchorage offer relief from the relentless swell and surf landings of the outer coast and good sheltered camping in stormy weather. This an-out-of-the way corner is seldom visited except by yachts seeking a sheltered anchorage. A main line logging road runs along the north shore of Klaskino Inlet and signs of logging are evident.

⊠↗ Brooks Peninsula Provincial Park – mile 40

Brooks Peninsula escaped glaciation 12,000 years ago, providing a refuge for flora and fauna while thick plates of ice scoured the rest of Vancouver Island. Consequently, the peninsula features a variety of rare plants and unusual geologic formations.

The peninsula creates its own local weather because of its exposure position on the northern end of Vancouver Islandand and its high mountains. Great care must be taken when venturing out. The isolation of the area adds further to the need for prudence.

Brooks Peninsula, northwest shore – mile 44

The north shore of Brooks Peninsula has some of the most rugged and exposed coastline on Vancouver Island. South of Orchard Point there are several beaches suitable for camping. The swell conditions and surf along the shore will dictate your choice. The first long sandy beach ends in a rocky headland that forms the northeast entrance to a lagoon. The southwest entrance to the lagoon is a tall sandy spit that provides some shelter on the

Rounding the Cape of Storms

Sheltered from wind-driven horizontal rain from a series of fast moving low-pressure systems, we have spent most of the last week in our tents. The urge to move on has become an obsession, and we are near desperate to round Cape Cook. Today has been a blustery day with successive late summer gales. Late in the day, we approach the corner of the beach closest to the cape. To our left, the surf curls in a nasty boat-breaking, plunging break. Ahead of us the right hand corner of the surf breaks less menacingly over outlying rocks close to shore where the water is deeper. During the lulls, there is fairly easy access to the corner of the beach. By silent mutual consent we land through the surf and set up our tents.

After dinner, I stand high on a log with my radio in order to tease in the VHF weather forecast. "With the passing of the cold front SE gales will back to NW 25 and rise to gales 35 in the afternoon." That, in a nut shell, is the north coast and is further confirmation of our dilema; north of the Brooks Peninsula is another world. If it is not blowing a gale in one direction it is blowing a gale in the opposite direction.

Conditions at Cape Cook, Cape of Storms are aggravated by the size and shape of Brooks Peninsula and Solander Island one mile offshore. The combined shoreline effects and gap winds routinely give Solander winds 15 knots greater than the general forecast. Northerly-flowing ocean currents accelerating over a shallow shelf further aggravate rising sea conditions.

The determination not to wait out the bad weather has practical ramifications. We will pre-pack the kayaks tonight, rise at 4:30 am and move out during any morning calm. If the sea rises through the night we will have to grin and bare it, breaking out of whatever is presented to us. Once around the cape at least the wind will be at our back and if sea conditions are not too bad it will be a quick trip. The evening is spent having a good meal and loading as much into the kayaks as possible. Days before I had found a flight feather from an eagle. Like a flag on the bow of a ship, it had been leading my way for the past few days. I pulled it out of its position and gently packed it below deck.

In the early morning there is good and bad news. The good news is that the breeze has remained light; the shore break in our sheltered corner is small. The bad news is that a dense fog has descended leaving us a bare 50 metres of visibility. Quietly we load the kayaks and line them three abreast along the beach ready for launch.

Each morning before leaving the beach, there is a moment of decision. Looking up at the sky and out to sea we must decide whether to remain in the safety of a well-made camp or venture out to sea. This morning we cannot see much sky or sea. Sliding into the cockpit, spray skirts on snapped on, we paddle out and accept the measured risks.

Away from the beach through a maze of rocks along the shore break, we turn left and paddle along the shore. We are paddling in the fog with a gale warning in force, heading for the Cape of Storms. Away from the beach, the morning breeze is out of the northwest at 15 knots with low swell. Keeping in sight of each other we paddle purposefully through the kelp beds keeping the steep rocky shore in view. The world is a monochrome of land, sea and sky. We should make the cape in about an hour. Following the indistinct shore, the compass swings from southwest to southeast as we round the Cape. Looking up from the compass a fog-bow has formed in our path. The bizarre appearance of this colourful portal to the southern world gives me more of a chill than can be accounted for by the fog alone. As we traverse the colourful arch the wind begins to build and the fog lifts a little. High over my left shoulder Cape Cook appears. To my right the foot of Solander Island briefly appears then, as if pulling a blanket over its toes, disappears.

Having turned the corner we look ahead to the southeast where the sky and sea are brilliant blue speckled by white clouds and wave crests. At sea level the wind is NW 20 and the waves are unexpectedly small; but we haven't escaped just yet. Low clouds forming over the three 300-metre summit of Cape Cook stream to the south at a remarkable pace. It is going to blow, hard, soon. Turning to Tom I say, "Let's get the hell out of here."

The threatening gale winds remain aloft and with fog, cloud and wind at our backs, it is a grand and joyous paddle. In just an hour we are looking ahead to Clerke Point. The swell offshore is breaking heavily over the shallow gravel banks and we pause to watch the surf, looking for any pattern or potential path along the shore inside the line of surf. Sneaking along the shore would save us from paddling a mile out to sea. The stiff wind at out back sails us forward as we continue to study the sets of breakers. Procrastination is itself a decision, and in time we drift into the shallows, successfully dodging smaller breakers and rocks. Only once was Tom left caught on a large boulder as a wave receded. Stranded he waited for the next hopefully not too large wave to release him.

Within 20 minutes of rounding the point, the swell and wind are reduced in the shelter of the peninsula. It had not been a long paddle but I had burnt whole day's nervous energy, my arms were heavy and I wanted to rest. Unfortunately there is no place for us to land.

After another hour and a half of paddling under the hot mid-day sun on calm seas we are able to land on a crescent beach of fine hot and dry white sand. Damp clothes and sleeping bags are pulled out and draped over logs and branches. For the first time in days we are warm and dry and having lunch in the shade of the trees.

inside. The next 3 miles are punctuated by several beaches with rocky headlands between them. From the last sandy beach approximately halfway between Orchard Point and Cape Cook, the shore is rocky and steep with little or no opportunity for landing.

Solander Island is one mile offshore from Cape Cook and the wind can be expected to be 10 to 15 knots higher than general conditions. The water is shallow and tidal current can add to the very demanding sea conditions.

Solander Island is an ecological reserve and landing is not permitted.

Brooks Peninsula – Cape Cook – mile 48

The west shore is exposed to good-weather northwest wind and bad-weather southeast winds; it is seldom a place to loiter.

The 5 mile-long western face of Brooks Peninsula rises 350 to 500 metres straight out of the water. Southwest winds accelerate as they progress along the face. A combination of vertical shore and shallow water out to sea can generate dangerous breaking and reflecting wave patterns. To further aggravate the situation, the shallow water offshore is strewn with large boulders and islets. The overall effect is a particularly rugged stretch of coastline. However, if you are fortunate enough to pass by during unusually calm weather when the swell is low or from the northwest, there are a few landing spots that are seldom visited.

Midway along the outer shore there is an isolated beach suitable for landing and camping. Fresh water is available. On a hot sunny day, north-west wind will funnel through the valley so expect strong gap winds. Most prudent paddlers on all but the most unusually calm days will likely not stop but instead continue on to the challenges of Clerke Point.

Clerke Point is low and wide with sizeable and irregular surf. Good judgement will allow you to either paddle out and around the line of outsurf or cut the corner through the shallow water near shore.

Brooks Peninsula – Clerke Point – mile 54

The south shore offers considerable shelter from the strong northwesterly fair-weather winds. After Clerke Point about 3 miles of rocky shores are punctuated by steep gravel and stone beaches. Then there are two beautiful sandy beachs sheltered behind some rocky islets. Dividing the beaches is a reliable creek offering fresh water making for a great beach camping.

Winter's southeasterly hurricane-force winds occasionally inundate this stretch; in 2003 a great deal of driftwood was flung beyond the tree line covering the established tent sites behind the edge of the forest.

Jacobsen Peninsula – mile 60

To the east, just before Jacobsen Peninsula, there is large open surf-swept beach. Once around Jacobsen Peninsula, tiny Peddler's Cove provides sheltered camping in all weather. Although it is occasionally inundated with driftwood, a good campsite can be found beneath the enormous Sitka spruce. Farther into the shelter of Columbia Cove are a few mooring buoys used by passing yachts and commer-

Morning on the east beach on Spring Island, Kyuquot.

cial fishing boats. There is a rough trail from Columbia Cove to the large surf-swept beach to the west.

Opportunities for relatively sheltered paddling exist to the east in Nasparti and Ououkinsh inlets and in Johnson Lagoon. The entrance to Johnson Lagoon is very narrow and the tidal current can be impassible; check tide and current tables for the time of slack water.

⌂ Acous Peninsula – mile 64

To the west are Acous Peninsula and Battle Bay, once principle village sites for the Checleset people.

The Acous Peninsula and the Bunsby Island group are in the heart of the Checleset Ecological Reserve and Checlescet/Kyuquot First Na-

tions territory. There are numerous Indian Reserves in the region and sensitive archaeological heritage sites. With increasing numbers of sea kayakers visiting the Bunsby Islands some camping sites are subject to considerable overuse. Information on appropriate campsites throughout the area can be obtained at the Checleset Kyuquot Band office.

In the Cuttle Islets there are campsites on the two larger islands with elevations reaching 70 and 125 metres.

To the northeast, Battle Bay is a large sandy beach and the northeastern portions are outside of the reserve and have suitable campsites on the beach. There is fresh water up Battle Creek beyond the estuary.

☐ Big Bunsby Marine Park – mile 67
Is located on Big Bunsby Island, near to Vancouver Island. The park is undeveloped and as a consequence most camping is outside the park. A popular sandy cove and campsite on the small island at the southeast entrance of Gay Passage is showing signs of overuse above the beach. The outermost island in the Bunsby group, has an elevation of 195 metres, Cautious Point has campsites for several tents.

Spring Island Recreation Site – mile 74
Once used as a military radar station, portions of Spring Island are now Forest Service Recreation Sites. The northeastern shallow beach is a popular camping area for trips starting or ending in Kyuquot. *West Coast Expeditions*, runs guided sea kayak trips from a base camp on the east end of this beach. When sea conditions permit, there are additional camping areas on top of the more exposed steeper gravel beaches to the west and south.

⌘☐↗ Kyuquot – mile 76
Kyuquot is located on Walter Island and is the northern terminus of the scheduled route of the *MV Uchuck III* out of Gold River. There is a community dock with a public telephone and a small store (the last time I was there it was open 1-6 pm). The one restaurant was open every day but more recently it has been open only

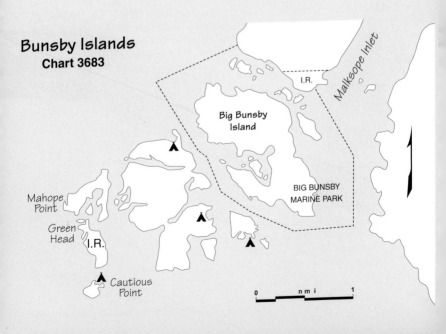

Bunsby Islands
Chart 3683

Malksope Inlet

I.R.

Big Bunsby
Island

BIG BUNSBY
MARINE PARK

Mahope
Point

Green
Head   I.R.

Cautious
Point

0   n m i   1

Sea Otters

Starting in 1741, lucrative and destructive northwest fur trade with its commercial harvest of sea otter pelts from Alaska to California was the beginning of the rapid near-extermination of a creature so vital to the health of the north Pacific coastal ecosystem.

These gentle creatures live on the open west coast in conditions more precarious than can be imagined. The red sea urchin is a favored food of the otter and the favored food of the red sea urchin is kelp. Populations of urchins left unchecked devour and destroy the kelp bed that is their home. The kelp provides an anchor point for a prolific web of life. When Vancouver Island's last sea otter was killed in 1929 an entire coastal ecosystem was spoiled. In many places today, the sea floor is barren where once there was lush kelp forest.

Between 1969 and 1972, approximately 100 sea otters were relocated from the Aleutian Islands to Checleset Bay north of Kyuquot. Checleset's remoteness, and abundant shallow reefs are ideal sea otter habitat. The sea otters have spread out from there and have been spotted from Cape Scott, to Clayoquot Sound. Recovery has been steady and the present population on Vancouver Island is estimated at around 2000.

To survive the cold-water these 60 to 80 pound mammals have the finest coat. A larger sea otter may have as many as a billion fur fibers. It is this most amazing coat that keeps the otter alive in the cold northeast Pacific Ocean. Guard hairs are about 1.5 inches long and the under-fur is a quarter inch shorter. Growing in bundles each with one guard hair and about 70 under-fur roots, a Sea Otter's coat is nearly twice as dense as a fur seal's coat.

one day a week to correspond to the *Uchuck's* schedule. On Thursday the *Uchuck* arrives with tourists who spend the night at a variety of bed and breakfast accommodations in Houpsitas village on the Vancouver Island shore just a few hundred yards away. The Indian village of Houpsitas is a community of about 300 people. There is a first aid station located on the Vancouver Island shore west of the village. Boat charters and a water taxi can be arranged out of Kyuquot or Houpsitas.

Short Excursions

Quatsino Sound

Accessed by road from either Winter Harbour (listed above) or Quatsino Provincial park/Spencer Cove Recreation Site, Quatsino Sound offers good paddling routes protected from the winds and ocean swell of the open coast. The Sound is also good starting point for excursions to the west coast.

⌂ Quatsino Provincial Park & Spencer Cover Recreation Site

Is an undeveloped park located on northern Quatsino Sound, on the east side of Koprino Harbour and

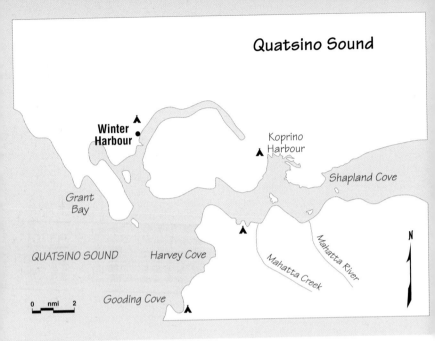

Quatsino Sound

Winter Harbour

Koprino Harbour

Shapland Cove

Grant Bay

QUATSINO SOUND   Harvey Cove

Mahatta Creek

Mahatta River

Gooding Cove

0   nmi   2

N

the adjacent peninsula to the east, as far as Shapland Cove and includes the Spencer Cove Recreation Site (11 campsites, a boat launch and a boat dock) in the shelter of Koprino Harbour. The Koprino River estuary is important fish and waterfowl habitat. The park is accessible by logging roads from Holberg.

Mahatta Creek

Gooding Cove, Kwakiutl Point, Raft Cove, Side Bay and the north shore of Brooks Peninsula are accessible by 2 or 3 days paddling from Quatsino Sound.

The inner waters of Quatsino Sound are extensive and offer a variety of kayaking opportunities away from the Pacific swells. Strong winds do blow up and down the inlet. Tidal currents in Quatsino Narrows run at up to 8 knots and must be paddled near slack water. The isolated village of Quatsino on the north shore near Quatsino narrows is home to approximately 100 people.

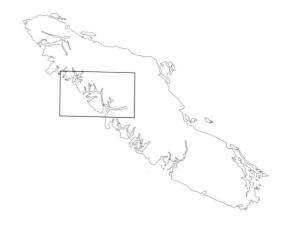

6

Kyuquot to Friendly Cove & Nootka Sound

Distance 46 nmi
Duration 4 travelling days
Charts #3675, #3676, #3682
Tides and Current Tables Vol. 6
Tide Reference Stations Tofino
Current Reference Stations not applicable
Weather Broadcast Region West Coast Vancouver Island South
Weather Reporting Stations Solander, South Brooks, Nootka
Coast Guard Services Kyuquot, Tahsis, Gold River, Tofino

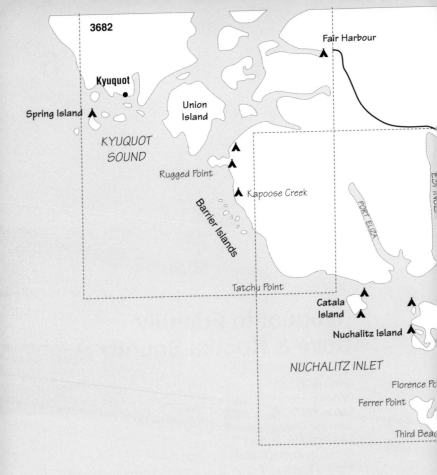

3682

Fair Harbour

Kyuquot

Spring Island

Union
Island

KYUQUOT
SOUND

Rugged Point

Kapoose Creek

Barrier Islands

PORT ELIZA

ESP...

Tatchu Point

Catala
Island

Nuchalitz Island

NUCHALITZ INLET

Florence Po...

Ferrer Point

Third Beac...

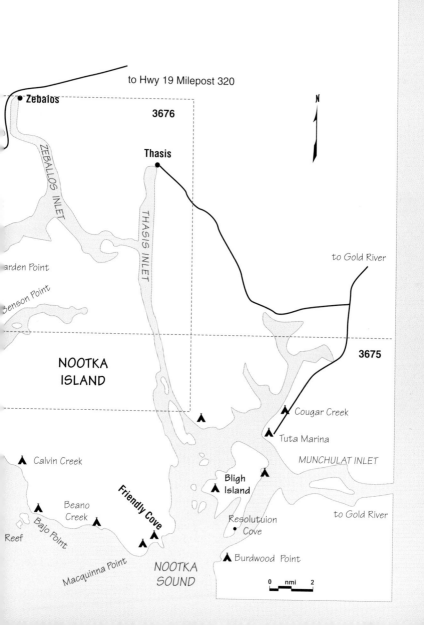

to Hwy 19 Milepost 320

• Zebalos

3676

Thasis

ZEBALLOS INLET

THASIS INLET

N

to Gold River

arden Point

Benson Point

NOOTKA
ISLAND

3675

Cougar Creek

Tuta Marina

Calvin Creek

MUNCHULAT INLET

Bligh
Island

to Gold River

Beano
Creek

Bajo Point

Friendly Cove

Resolutuion
Cove

Reef

Macquinna Point

NOOTKA
SOUND

Burdwood Point

0   nmi   2

The coastline from Kyuquot to Friendly Cove provides some the greatest diversity of coastal scenery on all of Vancouver Island. Exposed sections of coastline are interrupted by shallow headlands and groups of small islands that provide shelter and interest. Every few miles another spectacular beach invites landing and exploration. Inlets, sounds and island archipelagoes provide the opportunity for countless sheltered trips with good, although sometimes rough, road access. You can also access the area by sailing on the *MV Uchuck III* which provides freight and passenger to the coastal communites, and is by itself an attraction. There are several places that provide water taxis service. Wildlife is plentiful. Sea Otter colonies extend along the coast and I have encountered grey, humpback, minke, and orca whales in the region. I have also shared the beach with bears, cougars and wolves, thankfully never all at the same time. The weather is frequently better than that encountered north of the Brooks Peninsula.

Nootka Island is a cultural and historic focal point with a rich First Nation's and European history. A thriving culture developed magnificent ocean-going canoes still admired today. First Nations peoples of this region were effective whale hunters. Hunting such a large creature was dangerous but profitable, with each whale taken, providing the community with a vast amounts of food and resources. Whale hunting played a central roll in the life of the Nootka until the decline of traditional hunting in the late 1800s. Commercial whaling

began about the same time. In 1911, 1,200 whales were caught off the BC coast and as late as 1966 more than 700 whales were still being processed per year at coastal whaling stations. Now after a 35 year hunting moratorium, Grey and humpback whale populations are making a comeback.

In 1778, Captain James Cook was the first European to land on what are now the shores of British Columbia. The trade in seal and sea otter pelts made the area a center for international trade and the flash-point for hostilities between traders and native. Excessive hunting exterminated the local sea otter population but in the 1960's, sea otters were successfully reintroduced to the Bunsby Islands and can now be found from Cape Scott to Tofino.

The Nootka Island hiking trail that running from Louie Bay to Friendly Cove is becoming more popular every year. This wild coast of immense white sand beaches and forests of red cedar, Sitka spruce and hemlock is not a park and it does not have protected status. However, its increasing popularity may help secure it as a recreational area.

Paddling conditions

Beginners can experience guided trip in the Nuchatlitz Islands and the inner waters of Nootka Sound.

Intermediate paddlers can travel the inner water of Nootka Sound. With good local knowledge and some open water experience intermediate paddlers can reach the Nuchatlitz Islands and the Mission Group Islands near Kyuquot. When weather conditions are stable intermediate paddlers

Third Beach. Nookta.

can visit the outer coast beaches from Rugged Point 3-miles south to Mushroom Point.

Advanced paddling conditions exist across the windy open water of Kyuquot Sound. (Mushroom Point south to Tatchu Point is exposed with no easy landings. Tatchu Reef is shallow and hazardous with large surf and breaking waves well offshore.) The 2-miles of open water across Nuchatlitz Inlet can be windy and rough with some hazardous breaking waves well offshore. Ferrer Point is almost always rough with confused seas, due in part to a persistent northerly current running north across Tatchu Reef to the vicinity of Jurassic Point. From Ferrer Point south along the outer coast of Nootka Island is rugged coast interrupted with beautiful surf-swept beaches. Good weather, good judgement and advanced skill are required.

This region tends to have less vigorous weather conditions than the region north of Brooks Peninsula. Prevailing good summer weather conditions have strong winds from the northwest, so the preferred kayak routes are north to south. After a calm morning the wind will begin to rise as the sun warms the land. Northwesterly winds will be strong after noon and rise locally to gale force near the entrances of the sounds and inlets. Near sunset the wind will ease and change direction, flowing out of the inlets through the night. By morning, there should be calm conditions for another day of paddling. High cirrus clouds foretell a change in the

John Montgomery experiencing a 'wet-launch' from the deck of the Uchuck.

weather, and when the wind backs to any southern quadrant a storm is near and it is time to make camp. Fog banks can develop quickly at any time and reduce visibility to near zero; fortunately thay usually dissipate by the afternoon.

Safety considerations

The region is subject to predominantly advanced conditions with good opportunities for intermediate paddlers accompanied by an experienced leader familiar with the area. It Travel north to south in stable weather conditions. Mid July to mid August are best as these months have the driest and most stable weather.

Be self-reliant; the region is remote with few options for electronic communications. Camp on the many sheltered beaches and islands and wait for good sea conditions before continuing along the exposed sections of this coastline. In warm sunny conditions, the morning will be calm and the afternoon will be windy. When high clouds are followed by the wind backing to any southerly quadrant, you can anticipate a low-pressure weather system and potentially stormy wet weather.

Large ships enter Nootka Sound and travel the restricted waters to the paper mill in Thasis. The *Uchuck III* regularly travels a wide variety of routes between Gold River and Kyuquot. Near Kyuquot and Esperanza Inlet, there are frequent sport fishers and other small boat traffic.

Principle points of access

There are two good ways to access a coastal trip from Kyuquot to Friendly Cove: launch at Fair Harbour Recreation Site or take a trip on the *MV Uchuck III* from Gold River.

Road access to Fair Harbour and area

For road access to Fair Harbour at the north end of Nootka Island, drive 125 km north from Campbell River to the Zeballos turn-off. It is to your left at the 320 km marker post, 20 km past Woss. Woss is out of sight 200 m to the left. Stop there to top up your fuel tanks and check your spare tire before venturing onto the gravel roads.

There is a sign, 2 km prior to the Zeballos and Fair Harbour turn-off. Although the turn-off is well marked, it is hidden just beyond a bridge underpass. Turn left onto the gravel road and set your odometer to zero to help with your navigation. Signs along the road may be concealed by vegetation. Drive carefully, turn on your headlights and watch carefully for the signs.

Once on the gravel road, the first turn comes up quickly. After crossing the concrete bridge over the Nimpkish River, proceed up the hill and take the road to the right. Then 500 m farther along take the road to the left up the hill.

A few minutes later, you will encounter are some small bridges and then a fork in the road; watch the signs and stay to the right. At about 9 km take the left fork up the hill. The road twists and climbs to a summit at 22 km then descends into a valley. At

The Uchuck III

The *Uchuck* is one of the few remaining coastal freighters serving the remote villages and hamlets of Vancouver Island. The *Uchuck* name is derived from the local native language and means "Healing Waters." Built in 1942 as an American minesweeper, the *Uchuck* was later refitted to accommodate 100 passengers and up to 100 tons of cargo. It began passenger service in 1956. With a comfortable lounge, coffee shop and seating of the upper deck, a trip on the *Uchuck* is a relaxing way to spend a day. Remote logging camps, isolated villages, fish farms and sport fishing camps are supported by the regular run of the *Uchuck*. Crates of groceries, drums of fuel, steel cables and the occasional truck for a logging camp are typical cargo. Passengers aboard the *Uchuck* include kayakers with their boats, hikers, sightseers and local people going to work.

The *Uchuck* travels to Kyuquot once a week and runs other routes most days of the week. At 9 knots, the ship meanders comfortably along, taking a course out through Muchalat Inlet. The vast tree covered mountain inlets are interrupted with havens of habitation and industry tucked away in sheltered coves and bays where off-loading of freight accounts for a good portion of the ship's working day. Scheduled to arrive in Kyuquot in the late afternoon, the *Uchuck* will remain overnight before heading back to Gold River the next morning. Be patient—if there is a lot of freight to deliver the ship will adjust its schedule accordingly. It is all part of the adventure.

Steel-Grey Eyes in the Morning

It was a warm night on the beach at Calvin Creek. The air was cool and the heat the sun-warmed sand radiated from beneath the tent into my sleeping bag. The tent door was wide open to encourage the cool breeze to drift into the tent. With the Milky Way above and the luminescent white crests of the surf below, I fell asleep with my nose on the threshold of the tent. When next I opened my eyes I was staring directly into the steel-grey eyes of a large male wolf; I couldn't see the other five on the beach or hear the one in the woods behind my tent.

For a few seconds sight overwhelmed sound and I didn't hear Bob standing beside my tent yelling, "Hey wolf, go away wolf." I could see his shadow waving a paddle over his head trying to look big and scary. The first words out of my mouth were, "get your camera, get your camera!" However, I was to find out that Bob was in no mood to take time for snapshots.

I didn't know that minutes earlier Bob, having gone for a walk, spotted 7 wolves near the water's edge. When the wolves spotted Bob, they turned and began to trot in his direction. Totally exposed on

the beach with several wolves coming his way, Bob did not hesitate to make-good speed back to the campsite. His attempt to look big and scary did not seem to distract the lanky wolf's curiosity. In his own good time, the wolf ambled down the beach to meet up with the rest of the pack. Only then did Bob regain enough composure to tell his story while six wolves remained about 100 m down the beach.

I walk out on the beach to see the tracks and while busy looking around I heard the words, "Here they come…!" Sure enough, all 6 wolves, moving at a trot, were closing in; I scurried back to the security of my big scary friend. The pack stopped and watched us intently for a few seconds and then wandered back to their previous position on the beach. A rustling in the bush behind us gave away the position of the seventh member of the pack. All this time, a pup, too shy to cross in front of our camp, was stumbling through the bush trying to return to the pack. Soon the pup emerged from the forest and, once reunited, the pack turned and ambled away out of sight.

38 km you can turn left for the 3 km-long side road into Zeballos. Zeballos has a general store, marine supplies, a kayak shop and accommodations making it a good place to stop for last minutes supplies.

Fair Harbour Recreation Site

is 26 km beyond Zeballos. The site is undeveloped but provides ample camping, parking and good access

for exploring Kyuquot Sound and destinations along the west coast. Sport fishers use the site and residents of Kyuquot Village sometimes keep their vehicles there. From Fair Harbour it is about 10 nmi to paddle out to Rugged Point Provincial Park or Kyuquot Village on the west coast of Vancouver Island.

Logging roads are active with large logging trucks working Monday to

Friday until 6:00 pm. It is recommended that you drive active logging roads after 6:00 pm. There may be logging truck activity at any time and on weekends. Drive with your lights on and be prepared to yield. Carry at least one good spare tire. For more information on driving in and current road conditions please call Western Forest Product's office in Holberg.

MV Uchuck III

The *MV Uchuck III* is a pleasant and dust-free alternative to driving gravel logging roads. The *Uchuck* operates a regular freight and passenger service from the dock 10 km down the highway from Gold River. Along its 10-hour coastal route to Kyuquot, the *Uchuck* will drop you off just about anywhere the ship can stop in calm water. I highly recommend this excellent and affordable service.

You can also launch kayaks from the boat ramp next to the dock where the *Uchuck III* is tied up.

You can make reservations to spend the night at a B&B in the village or arrange to camp on some local property. Another alternative is to paddle 3 nmi to Spring Island Recreation Site and camp on the beach.

Coastal trip

⌂ ↗ ◆ Kyuquot – mile 0

is a community consisting of Houpsitas Village and an adjacent hamlet on Walter Island. On Walter Island there is a government dock, telephone, general store, post office, restaurant and some marine facilities. The store may be open only a few hours each day and the restaurant may not be open at all.

There is a Red Cross medical clinic along the shore near Houpsitas Village. Bed and breakfasts and private camping are available at Houpsitas Village and on Walter Island.

⌂ ↗ Spring Island Recreation Site – mile 2

is one of the mission group islands and was once leased to the United States military for a radar station. The overgrown roadbed and beach is now a Forest Service Recreational area with good camping opportunities. The area's most sheltered and most frequently used site is the shallow bay on the eastern shore. Other beaches offer more seclusion, better views and more exposure to the weather. Several of the adjacent islands are part of an Indian reserve. If you are in doubt, check at the band office in Houpsitas Village. *West Coast Expeditions* has a base camp on Spring Island and they can be contacted for water taxi service.

⌂ Rugged Point Provincial Marine Park – mile 7

is undeveloped with easy landing in the well-used sheltered bay at the park's northwest end. A path leads from the bay across the headland to more exposed western beaches.

Aptly named, the point is rugged and exposed to the ocean swell. Intrepid paddlers can head south to land their kayaks through the surf and camp on a series of fine sandy beaches. Although the Barrier Islands do not stop the incoming Pacific swell entirely, the sea conditions along the more southerly beaches are eased greatly. The beaches are frequented by only a few visitors, and you are likely to have a mile of sand all to yourself. There are a few rough and exposed camping stops on the outer islands for the wind-hardy camper. Sea otters inhabit the kelp beds, and catching fish for lunch is not likely to take very long. Water is available in McLean Cove 0.5 miles northeast of Rugged Point.

⊡ ≈ Kapoose Creek – mile 9

You can walk trails across the headlands or paddle to the beach at Kapoose Creek. With the summit of Remarkable Cone rising behind the expanse of white sand beach, this spot is spectacular. You can paddle up creek to fetch fresh water.

⌘ ≈ Jurassic Point – mile 13

marks the end of the sandy beaches and shelter from the Barrier Islands and the beginning of steep gravel beaches exposed to uninterrupted swell. The steep gravel makes landing suitable only on days when the swell is near one metre. True to its name, the surrounding area has fossil evidence of prehistoric life. Wrangellia is a geologic terrain that encompasses Vancouver Island, Haidi Gwaii (the Queen Charlotte Islands) and southeast Alaska. Please leave all fossils in place and undisturbed (refer to *West Coast Fossils*).

⊠ Tatchu Point – mile 15

The waters off Tatchu Point are shallow and exposed to uninterrupted swell. A combination of shallow water, large waves and the confounding effects of any headland, produce an area of frequent large boomers

extending well offshore. Take great care passing Tatchu Point. Although we have passed by Tatchu Point close to shore and well inside most of the surf, we have also had some amazing rides on very large unexpected waves. The best advice is to swing a wide course offshore and keep a good lookout for shallow spots with large breaking waves. Once you turn onto an easterly course through Rolling Roadstead, the swell will roll but will not break nearly so often. Sea conditions should ease considerably as you enter Esperanza Inlet past Yellow Bluff, and approach Catala Island. There are nice gravel beaches along the north shore of Rolling Roadstead and good water from the river near Peculiar Point.

⊡ Nuchatlitz Provincial Marine Park – mile 22

is located at the northwest entrance to Nuchatlitz Inlet and offers a variety of paddling opportunities and an excellent introduction to paddling the west coast of Vancouver Island. You will find exposed coast with ocean swell breaking on rough rocky shore and protected waters with quiet coves and beaches. Undeveloped but useable camping areas are scattered throughout the park. See below for opportunities for short excursions in Nuchatlitz Provincial Marine Park.

⊡ ↗ Catala Island – mile 18

is located at the entrance to Esperanza Inlet and lies within Nuchatlitz Provincial Marine Park. There is abundant good camping high on the gravel beaches. The *Uchuck* can launch or pickup kayakers here. After a warm

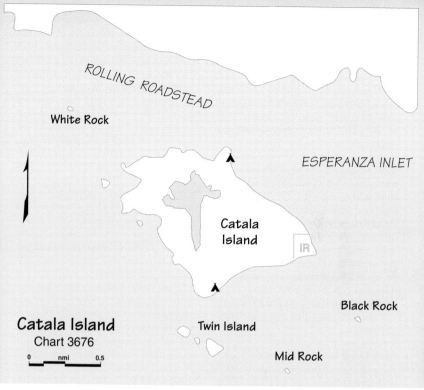

ROLLING ROADSTEAD

White Rock

ESPERANZA INLET

Catala
Island

IR

Black Rock

Catala Island
Chart 3676

0   nmi   0.5

Twin Island

Mid Rock

day there is often a strong nightly out-flow wind. Set up your tent and tarp up for a change in wind direction or else you will be up at 2 am adjusting poles and guy-lines. The noises you hear the middle of the night are likely to be deer browsing in the open grass behind the beach. The area around Catala Island is worth investigating for a few days, with sheltered pad-dling on the inside and open coastal paddling on the outside through kelp beds and rock gardens. Catala is a good location for a base camp before to venturing down the west coast of

Nootka or into more sheltered waters of Esperanza and Nuchatlitz Inlets.

Nootka Island Trail

The 53 km Nootka Island Trail on the west coast of Nootka Island runs through beautiful forest and along several long beaches. The northern trailhead is in Louie Bay, located between Florence Point and Ferrer. In the south the trail ends at Yuquot (Friendly Cove). The trail is becoming increasingly popular but is not regu-larly maintained. Along the way the trail crosses six Indian Reserves. Fees may be in charged to camp in Yuquot or to pass through the other reserves.

☒ Ferrer Point – mile 26

marks the beginning to the unsheltered west coast of Nootka Island and the northern end of the Nootka Island Trail. A slight but steady current runs by the point contributing to frequent rough sea conditions. The area is a popular salmon fishing spot for local sport fishers. They skirt the chaos of waves In small boats, bouncing off the shallow bottom and the rocky shore. Shallow waters, rebound waves and a steady current create rough sea conditions and good judgment and fair weather are needed when rounding Ferrer Point. Ferrer Point to Third Beach is a magnificent rugged paddle with no place to land until Third Beach. Signs of shipwreck are clearly visible along this unforgiving stretch of coastline.

⌂ ≋ Third Beach – mile 29

is the first available landing site south of Ferrer Point. Approaching Third Beach from the north there is access through the rocks to a small sheltered west facing beach. Alternately the main beach can be approached from the south. Approaching from the south, the surf at Third Beach dumps close to shore; use the westernmost corner of the beach for a softer landing. Once onshore, investigate the area near the center of the beach, where winter storms have blasted sand well back into the trees; a testament to the ferocity of winter gales. If you want a less sandy tentsite you can move up to the grassy terrace behind the beach. There is usually water running from the creek on the east end of the beach where the trail comes down from the forest. The beach at Calvin Creek is another 5 nmi along the coast. On the way you will pass a steep beach at Skuna Bay, and if you stop there you will probably be all alone. However, it is usually preferable to continue south to the splendid beach at Calvin Creek.

⌂ ≋ Calvin Creek – mile 34

Crawfish Falls is at the center of a magnificent sandy beach. From a mile away, you can see the cascade of water six metres tall and ten metres wide. There is a good sized swimming hole beneath the waterfall. Even on the calmest days, there is no avoiding some surf at Calvin Creek. The surf is largest when the swell direction is from the west to southwest. A shallow reef off the northern entrance to the beach takes the edge of the surf when the swell comes in from the west or northwest. You will have to paddle south and remain offshore almost to the middle of the beach before turning northeast to approach the beach. From your campsite on the beach the surf rolling in under the evening sunset is a remarkable sight. Fossilized leaves, 30 million year old, are visible on the slabs south of the falls. A few local charter pilots land helicopters and small planes on the expanse of flat sand but can stay only an hour or two during the lowest tides.

Alex Matthews at Calvin Creek, Crawfish Falls.

⊠ ◁ ≈ Bajo Point – mile 36

Bajo Reef extends 3 nmi out to sea creating a formidable obstacle to navigation. Fortunately, as the tide rises there is sufficient depth for kayaks to pass inside the inner reef, protected from surf breaking over miles of shallow rocks. The approach to the inner passage is not apparent, but continue to paddle along the shore and the route will open up. The 40 foot-tall obelisk of rock on the inner reef clearly marks the way. The inside route is just inshore of that rock with another route close to seaward of the rock. Once you are through the inner passage, Bajo Reef provides shelter from northwesterly winds and swell. Camping is available at Bajo Point among giant spruce trees. There is scant evidence of a once well-established native village in the forest.

◁ ≈ Beano Creek – mile 40

runs through a steep gravel berm and may not be visible from seaward; however it is not hard to see where the creek runs through the trees. The western approach is a flat gravel beach, and the eastern approach is very steep gravel. The mouth of the creek is often dammed by gravel, forming a large freshwater pool perfect for swimming. A well-kept cabin is tucked behind a row of trees overlooking the creek, and there are usually a few campers about. From Beano Creek you can see Maquinna Point and the entrance to Nootka Sound in the distance.

⊠ Maquinna Point – mile 43

has steep cliffs that reflect the incoming swell and create irregular and sometimes difficult sea conditions.

You may find gentler sea conditions by moving offshore away from the zone of reflected waves. Once around the point, expect sea conditions to improve. The shore becomes a maze of rocks and kayak-sized passages fun for exploring. The cliffs provide a spectacular scene cut with many small caves and rock formations. The swell reflects off the cliffs and sea conditions can be irregular well offshore. As the shoreline turns in toward Nootka Sound the rock formations continue and the exposure to north-westerly sea conditions is reduced. It is a wonderful place to paddle along the shore in amongst the rock pillars and sea-arches. Friendly Cove (Yuquot) is around the corner past a nice beach and a tidal lagoon.

Found 1.5 nmi northeast of Maquinna Point is a camping area above the beach on the east side of the mouth of the estuary. From there you can still see the open Pacific to the south and the long gravel beach and church at Friendly Cove to the east.

Another 1.5 miles brings you to Nootka lighthouse on San Rafael Island. This picturesque beacon is one of the last remaining manned lighthouses on the BC Coast. Friendly Cove is just around the corner.

⌘ ⊡ ≈ ↗ Friendly Cove (Yuquot) – mile 46

The local native band charges a modest landing fee, and there is easy camping in a variety of locations within the reserve. Walk the polished pebble beaches or swim in the lake. If you have time, rent one of the cabins along the lake or oceanfront and spend a day in Yuquot.

Beano Creek, Nookta. Creek water backs up behind the gravel berm making for great swimming.

Captain James Cook Lands at Friendly Cove

In July 1776, Captain James Cook sailed from England to these shores in search of the much sought-after Northwest Passage. Two years later in March 1778, his ships reached Nootka Sound where Cook went ashore at the southern end of Nootka Island. Although explorers had been in these waters before, most had stayed in their ships trading from offshore. Arriving at Friendly Cove, Cook was the first European step onto what is now known as British Columbia. Maquinna, the heredity Chief of the local Indian band was there to greet him. Cook's two ships, Resolution and Discovery, remained anchored for a month in a cove off a nearby island. Here Cook took advantage of local resources to replace two of his masts. Today Resolution Cove takes its name from Cook's ship and the island takes its name—Bligh Island—from one of Cook's crew. Bligh served as a navigator aboard the Resolution and gained infamy years later as Captain Bligh of "Mutiny on the Bounty." After the initial meeting between European and West Coast Natives, the fur trade reached such proportions that within a few decades populations of sea otter, fur seal and beaver were nearly exterminated. In subsequent years, relations between Europeans and the local natives were not always friendly. Trade also brought conflict between the British and the natives. In 1803 a new Chief attacked a British trading ship from Boston killing all but two of its crew. The survivors were kept as slaves for more than 2 years. Years later in 1815, one of the survivors, John Rogers Jewitt, wrote the story of their ordeal, *White Slaves of Maquinna*.

Simultaneously, thousands of miles away in Europe, a war between England and Spain almost broke out over rights to plunder the rich timber and fur on BC's coast. Local conditions provoked by international trade were largely responsible for the decimation of the BC coast's native population from approximately 50,000, to 15,000 by 1935. There are visible reminders of this 200-year-old history. Brass plaques on the rocks at Resolution Cove commemorate Cook's landing.

A donation will get you a guided tour of the church and the site. When I was there our guide was a descendent of Chief Maquinna who met Captain Cook near this site. The church is an eclectic mix of native and European influences. The church features totem poles flanking the alter facing a sculpture of a killer whale at the other end. An articulated thunderbird dominates overhead while traditional Spanish stained glass windows adorn the front doors.

From here, it is 22 nmi up Muchalat Inlet to Gold River. The *Uchuck* provides service to Friendly Cove three times a week, and if you have a reservation or space is available you can board the *Uchuck* for a pleasant ride back to Gold River. Alternately, the inner reaches of Nootka Sound provide miles of shoreline to explore.

Yuquot at Friendly Cove

The ancient village of Yuquot has been settled continuously for over 4,300 years and was once populated by 1,500 natives in about 20 wooden longhouses. This is the only region in Pacific Canada where natives have hunted whales. One of the most significant archaeological finds associated with this heritage is known as the 'Whalers Shrine.' Originally located at one of the lakes adjacent to Yuquot, the shrine was dismantled in 1905, removed and taken to the American Museum of Natural History in New York. Negotiations are in progress to repatriate the shrine to the village of Yuquot.

Word of the fur trade reached the Spaniards in Mexico. The Viceroy decided to assert Spain's sovereignty and establish a fort and church adjacent to Friendly Cove. It was Spain's northernmost garrison in the Pacific and the only one established in Canada. Trade disputes led Britain and Spain to the brink of war, and Spain reluctantly backed down in 1790.

To celebrate the bicentennial of the historic meeting between Captains Vancouver and Quadra, Spain donated a commemorative stained glass window to the village for the Roman Catholic Church which was originally built in 1789.

Yuquot is now a National Historic Site. By 1970, all but one native family had left the village. Most of the other inhabitants had moved to Vancouver Island. In summer, however, the village still sees its share of activity. In Aug 2003, Yuquot hosted the North Vancouver Island native games, with over 300 visitors and participants.

⌂✣ Bligh Island – mile 49

is named after Captains Cook's infamous navigator. On the southwestern end there is a user maintained camping area on the isthmus opposite Clotchman Island. This is a popular spot so expect to find other kayak campers there. Vernaci Island, a mile to the west has a small camp area. There are other undeveloped wilderness sites in the adjacent Spanish Pilot Group of islands.

In Resolution Cove there are two brass plaques placed to commemorate Cook's landing in 1776.

Recreation sites at Cougar Creek and Tuta Marina can be accessed by road from Tlupana Inlet. From Gold River, the well maintained gravel road to Tahsis begins about 3 km past the Gold River Travel Info Centre. About 25 km along the road take the left turn to Tlupana Inlet. From the turn-off, it is about 15 km to Cougar Creek and another 5 km to Tuta Marina.

Short excursion

Nuchatlitz Islands – chart #3676

Nuchatlitz Islands Provincial Marine Park is situated on the north shore of Nootka Island at the entrance to Esperanza Inlet. The islands can be accessed by water taxis from Zeballos, Thasis or by the *Uchuck III* sailing out of Gold River. The intrepid paddler can also paddle out under their own steam. The area is great for wildlife viewing; there are sea otters and eagles offshore, and bears, wolves and cougars onshore. The rugged, intricate shoreline interrupted by many small beaches provides endless opportunity for exploration.

Inside the church at Friendly Cove—a mix of European and native cultures.

Paddling conditions

Nuchatlitz Islands are well suited for sea kayaking and the proximity of sheltered islets in full view of the open Pacific makes the Nuchatlitz Islands a popular destination for guided trips. To the northeast, Esperanza Inlet provides many miles of west coast paddle away from rolling Pacific swell.

Safety considerations

Intermediate to advanced conditions with good opportunities for beginners with a skilled leader or guide.

While many small islets provide considerable shelter, imprudent kayakers can get themselves into a good deal of trouble if they venture out to where the pacific swells break heavily over the outer shores. Passage into Nuchatlitz Inlet can be deceptively challenging as wave heights build and steepen over shallow waters.

Principle points of access

From the road to Fair Harbour (see above) you can either launch out of Zeballos and paddle 20 miles out of Zeballos Inlet or continue about 7 km past Zeballos to Little Espinosa Recreation Site at the head of Little Espinosa Inlet adjacent to the bridge. You will have to park on or near the road. Time your departure through the tidal rapid to coincide with slack water and then paddle the 6 miles out to Garden Point Recreation Site on Nootka Island. To cross Esperanza Inlet there is a mile of open water from the entrance of Espinosa Inlet to Nootka Island. Access to the Nuchatlitz Islands is easy.

You can get water taxis service from Zeballos or Thasis. Leaving by ship from Gold River, the *MV Uchuck III*

The Uchuck III in Friendly Cove. Photo: Gillean Daffern.

can launch or pick you up at Garden Point or Rosa Island

⌂✗ Nuchatlitz Provincial Marine Park

This park is undeveloped with good camping on Catala (above) and Rosa Island. The park has numerous small islets, reefs, privately own islands and Indian reserves. Within the park are a number of archaeological sites. The islands offer a contrast of exposed coasts, quiet coves, tide pools and a multitude of beaches. There are a sheltered camping areas on several of the small islands. If sea state or westher conditions build you can head into the sheltered waters of Esperanza Inlet.

Venturing south across Nuchatlitz Inlet to Louie Bay, there is a camp area south of Florence Point and the remains of a radar station near Tongue Point. In Starfish Lagoon, located south of Louie Bay, a path leads across a narrow neck of land from the tip of the lagoon to a lovely sandy beach locally known as Third Beach. Seaplanes land in Louie Bay to drop off hikers starting the Nootka Trail.

✗⌂♨ Little Espinosa Recreation Site – mile 0

is a small day-use site with a rough boat launch good for launching trips to Esperanza Inlet and the Nuchatlitz Islands. It is located 7 km along the gravel road beyond Zeballos Lagoon.

⌂∾✗ Garden Point Recreation Site – mile 6

There are tent sites on the sand and pebble beach at the mouth of Brodick Creek and more sites in the adjacent old growth forest. This is a popular and well-used camping area. In the past irresponsible campers have

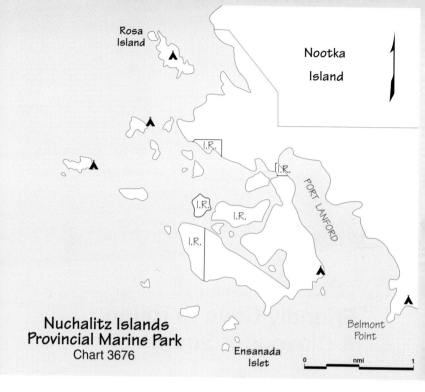

Nootka Island

Rosa Island

I.R.

I.R.

I.R.

I.R.

I.R.

PORT LANFORD

Belmont Point

Ensanada Islet

Nuchalitz Islands Provincial Marine Park
Chart 3676

0   nmi   1

caused problems with bears by leaving around. Most recently, however, camping has been safe and undisturbed.

⌂ ∿ ↗ Rosa Island – mile 9

There is a popular camp area in the trees behind a small sandy beach on the island's southeast corner. The *Uchuck* can stop here to launch or pick up kayakers. In the westernmost part of the Nuchatlitz Islands, several islets have small campsites.

Nuchatlitz Inlet – mile 13

There are areas to camp on Nootka Island at Belmont Point at the entrance to Nuchatlitz Inlet just prior to entering Port Langford, and a very popular spot on the "Grassy Knoll" northeast of Ensanada Islet.

If you are exploring the reaches of Nuchatlitz Inlet be wary of swell from the west. The shoreline east from Belmont Point to Benson Point and the shallow entrance to Nuchatlitz Inlet can be subject to large waves. In calm conditions, the inlet is peaceful and leads into the shelter of Mary Basin, however, the entrance to the inner basin is subject to very strong tidal currents, enter with caution.

7

Friendly Cove to Tofino
& Clayoquot Sound

Distance 50 nmi
Duration 4 travelling days
Charts #3673, #3674, #3675
Tides and Current Tables Vol. 6
Tide Reference Stations Tofino
Current Reference Stations not applicable
Weather Broadcast Region West Coast Vancouver Island South
Weather Reporting Stations Nootka, Estevan Point, Tofino, Leonard Island,
    La Perouse Bank, Amphitrite Point
Coast Guard Services Gold River, Tofino

The low featureless ground of Hesquiat Peninsula separates Nootka and Clayoquot sounds. Extending 15 miles north to south, the peninsula is fringed by long sandy beaches and extensive kelp beds. The region has a mild wet climate with less frequent severe weather than regions farther north. Sea otters poke their heads out as you paddle by and grey whales sedately pass by on their 10,000-mile northerly migration. The splendid lighthouse at Estevan Point holds claim as being the only lighthouse to be bombarded by a submarine during WWII.

Hesquiat Harbour is open to the southwest and provides only minimal shelter for paddlers. Boat Basin at the head of the harbour provides some sheltered anchorage in all but the worst weather and small boats can seek refuge in the tiny enclosure of Rae Basin. At the very highest tide a kayak may be able to be paddled into Hesquiat Lake. The region from Hesquiat south to Tofino is known as Clayoquot Sound.

The Nuu-chah-nulth people are the original inhabitants of Clayoquot Sound. With their support this area of coastal temperate rainforest has been designated as a UNESCO Biosphere Reserve. This designation incorporates the three functions of conservation, sustainable development and research.

Just a few decades ago, logging and fishing were the predominent activities around Clayoquot Sound. There are no established coastal roads in the area. A few logging roads reach the shore but most do not join with any other central road on Vancouver Island. Boats still remain the main mode of transportation. Arriving from

Luna the killer whale rubbing against a small boat at Gold River docks.

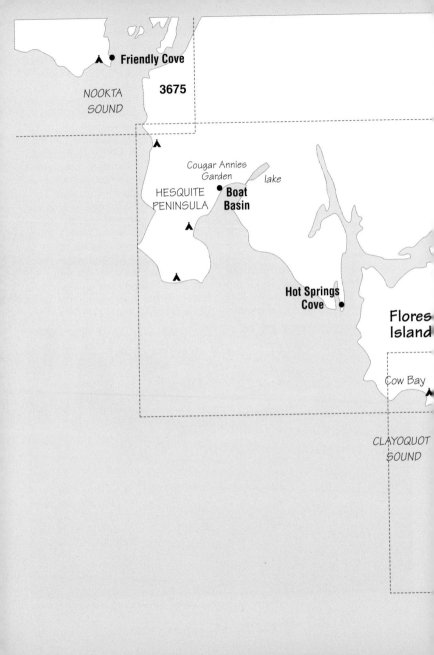

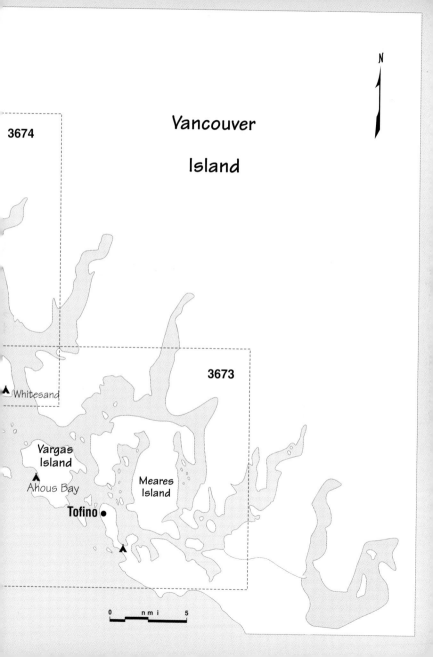

MV Uchuck III underway in Esperanza Inlet.

the north, the paved road at Tofino is the first you will have encountered in 225 miles since Port Hardy on the northeast coast of Vancouver Island.

Good summer weather attracts tens of thousands of ecotourists, surfers and paddlers to the busy seaside cottages, R.V. sites and campgrounds near Tofino and Ucluelet. Violent winter storms and the huge Pacific swell they generate are also a tourist attraction, enticing weather-watchers to reserve hotels rooms and cabins overlooking the shore. Today, tourism draws an international hustle and bustle of cars, boats and seaplanes to an otherwise isolated coastal village.

Paddling Conditions
Beginners can travel with an experienced leader through the more sheltered waters of Clayoquot Sound. At times some of the more sheltered areas are open to swell and many of the inland passages of Clayoquot Sound have swift currents. Fog and frequent small boat traffic add significant hazards to travelling the region. Experience and good judgement are necessary throughout the area.

Intermediate paddlers with good local knowledge can travel the inside waters of Clayoquot Sound. The outer shores of Vargas and Flores islands are fully exposed with rocky headlands and surf-swept beaches. Summer conditions often allow for intermediate paddlers to accompany an experienced leader along these dramatic shores. This popular area has ready access to water taxi service and VHF radio communications.

Advanced paddling conditions predominate the coast from Friendly Cove to Tofino. Open-water crossings and long stretches of coast provide few easy landing opportunities. Declining weather conditions can create significant hazards along any portion of the outer coast. During times of bad sea conditions the shallow reefs offshore can limit the access to the shelter of Hesquiat Harbour, Sydney Channel and the eastern shore of Vargas Island. Tidal current outflows from the inlets of Clayoquot Sound add to the possibility of hazardous sea conditions in offshore waters. Good local knowledge and judgement are necessary when traveling this dynamic and complex stretch of shoreline.

The same complexity that creates potential hazards can offer shelter to the experienced. Touring during times of moderate weather provides spectacular scenery and the opportunity for wilderness camping and splendid coastal adventures. There are numerous water taxi services for ease of access and VHF radio communications are effective, with numerous other boats and commercial traffic in the region.

Safety Considerations

- Large ships travel in and out of Nootka Sound. Crossing Nootka Sound is advised only in clear conditions.
- The numerous beaches along the west of Hesquiat Peninsula and the entire western shore of Clayoquot Sound are subject to surf.
- The shores along Hesquiat Peninsula are shallow and extend a long way offshore. Swell can form isolated surf waves (boomers) over the area's many rocky reefs.
- Hesquiat Bar is shallow and exposed to southerly storm weather. Swell from any southerly direction can form large breaking waves that stretch across the full width of Hesquiat Harbour.
- The entrance to Sydney Inlet is subject to strong tidal current and when ebb currents encounter westerly winds steep and irregular rough seas can form in the vicinity of Sharp Point.
- The west shore of Flores Island is rugged and exposed with few easy landing opportunities. Rafael Point is well known for locally rough and changing sea conditions and has been the site of a number of sea kayak incidents involving large seas and poor judgment.
- Cow Bay is subject to surf in southwesterly swell conditions.
- The 3-mile crossing from Flores Island to Vargas Island is strewn with rocks and islets with hazardous breaking waves.
- The southwest shore of Vargas is shallow and rock strewn well offshore. Large waves form over the innumerable small reefs. Tidal outflows from Father Charles Channel can create steep and confused seas during times of westerly winds.
- Clayoquot Sound sees a lot of commercial boat traffic, particularly small high-speed boats. Fog is common, and during times of low visibility the amount of boat traffic creates a significant hazard. Stay onshore and wait for better visibility; if you must travel, announce your

position on VHF radio channel 16, carry a radar reflector and stay very close to shore whenever possible.

Principle points of access

The inside waters of Nootka Sound are accessible from Cougar Creek and Tuta Marina (see section 6). Launching from either of these spots or from Gold River adds a full day of paddling to this route and a difficult return trip to pick-up vehicles.

From Gold River you can launch kayaks from the boat ramp next to the dock where the *Uchuck III* is tied up or take a ride on the *Uchuck*. A good choice is to have the *Uchuck* drop you off in Mooyah Bay, 5 miles up Muchalat Inlet northeast of Burdwood Point. If you have left a second vehicle in Tofino you can shuttle back to Gold River at the end of the trip.

If you are tired or the fog is too persistent, water taxi service can be hired from Hot Springs Cove. There is enough commercial boat traffic along the main waterways of Clayoquot Sound that water taxis can usually be contacted on the VHF radio.

At the south end of the trip, the government dock at the end of 1st Street in Tofino provides easy access for paddlers.

Tofino

The busy village of Tofino is located on the east side of Esowista Peninsula. Clayoquot Sound is the traditional territory of the Tla-o-qui-aht, Ahousaht and Hesquiat First Nations. The First Nations community of Opitsaht, is about one mile across the Tofino harbour on Meares Island. Meares Island is renowned for its enormous

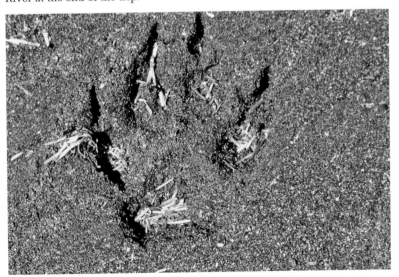

Bear tracks in coarse sand.

red cedars and 1,500-year-old Sitka spruce trees. The shallow waters surrounding Meares Island are swept by quickly moving currents exposing extensive mudflats at low tide.

The town of Ucluelet is 33 km south of Tofino by road. Here paddlers can gain access to the northern reaches of Barkley Sound and the scheduled ferry routes of the MVs Lady Rose and Francis Barkley that operate between Port Alberni, Barkley Sound, Bamfield and Ucluelet.

Tsunami

At 8.4 on the Richter scale, the earthquake of March 27, 1964 near Anchorage Alaska was the largest ever recorded in the Northern Hemisphere. The earthquake resulted in 520,000 square kilometers of ground being vertically displaced by more than 10 meters. This massive displacement generated a devastating tsunami which reached a maximum wave height of 67 meters at Valdez Inlet. The wave traveled throughout the Pacific basin and caused considerable damage on the west coast of Vancouver Island. The tide gauge at Tofino recorded a 1.2 metre rise but the effects of the wave running up over shallow water were considerably greater. Local accounts focussed on significant damage that occurred in Port Alberni and spoke little about the devastation to remote low-lying coastal communities. Villages at the heads of shelving inlets such as Hesquiat Harbour, Hot Springs Cove and Zeballos suffered quite badly. At Hot Springs Cove 16 of its 18 homes were destroyed, and in Zeballos 30 dwellings were moved off their foundations.

Coastal trip

Friendly Cove mile 0

The *Uchuck*, leaving from Gold River, can drop you off in Friendly Cove. There is good camping on the reserve and it is a great spot to visit. Walk up to the house attached to the church and pay your camp fee before you pick a spot to set up a tent.

If you have been to Friendly Cove before or if you want to avoid crossing Nootka Sound you can have the *Uchuck* drop you off in Muchalat Inlet near Mooyah Bay. From there paddle the 5 nmi along the northwest shore of Hesquiat Peninsula to Burdwood Point.

⌂ Burdwood Point mile 2.5

It is a 2 mile open-water crossing from Friendly Cove to Burdwood Point. Afternoon winds funnel into Nootka Sound and there is sport fishing activity in the areas. Although quite sheltered, the bay and sandy beach adjacent to Burdwood Point can be subject to surf conditions.

Hesquiat Peninsula Provincial Park

Hesquiat Peninsula Provincial Park comprises most of the shore of Hesquiat Peninsula and extends from Escalante Point to Hesquiat Lake in Rae Basin. There are several First Nations reserve lands within the general park area. The peninsula is low and featureless and the sea depths offshore are shallow, with waves cresting and booming over many isolated rocks. The entire peninsula is exposed to Pacific weather and swell, and the many long sandy beaches are all subject to surf conditions. Camping

It's 24 miles from here

We had bivouacked peacefully in Homais Cove. As usual the day's times and distances paddled were duly recorded before making a paddling plan for tomorrows departure to Hot Springs Cove. With the chart on the sand I measured off the distance to be paddled by outstretching my index finger and little finger on my right hand. The span represents one hours paddling; a measurement confirmed after many seasons and hundreds of mile of coastal touring, one – two – three – four – aaand a half. "It is about four and half-ish hours to Hot Springs." I reported.

The glass-calm morning foretold the hot and breathless day to follow. Paddling across the wide mouth of Hesquiat Bay was a chore with no place to land from start to finish. At two-o-clock we landed at the dock greeted by the wharfinger. "Hi, are you Dave, Don in Tofino asked me to say hello." "Yeah, I'm Dave where have you come from?" he replied. "We left Homais this morning and paddle straight here with nowhere to stop."

"Now that's quite a paddle, 24 miles without a break."

"Well it's more like 14 miles but in today's heat it felt like 24." I said.

To make a rather long story short, to confirm his navigational expertise Dave took us onto in his yacht where he disconnected the fax machine, and the radiotelephone in order to reconnect the global positioning satellite navigation system. He then proceeded to up-load the software for the local chart. "I will mark your course in along the rocks near shore. It will give us a more accurate measurement." He said with great technical confidence.

You see, including the time spent for drink breaks, snack stops, conversation, and wildlife viewing opportunities, we travel at a fraction over 3 knots. That is what my log book consistently records for the last many years and many hundreds of miles. Arriving at the dock, before exiting the kayak, I looked at my watch and wrote on my slate, Arr Hot Springs 14:15 pm. The line before read Lv Homais 09:20. Now that's 5 hours at 3+ knots for a distance of 15+ miles. In reporting to Dave our distance traveled of 14 miles I took off a mile because I thought in the hot conditions we were probably just a little slow today.

Dave was poised to display his electronic solution, "Now this will tell us exactly how far you traveled." And he depressed the appropriate button. The digital output read 14.4 miles. "Ummmm, that's interesting" Dave conceded.

A chart, outstretched fingers, a watch and notes kept on a waterproof slate, have served well for navigating a kayak along many coastal routes.

is permitted throughout the park. No facilities are available.

⌂ Escalante Point – mile 5
There are many good campsites along the 3 km of flat sand along Escalante Beach. Some portions of the beach are exposed to swell and surf but other spots are sheltered by small offshore islands. The Escalante River has many great freshwater pools for swimming.

⌂ Barcester Bay – mile 10
More large sandy beaches invite landing through the surf at Barcester Bay. Both the headland 2 miles south, and Homais Cove are part of a reserve and once the site of an ancient village. Homais Cove is a strategic spot to camp before crossing Hesquiat Bar. Plan ahead and ask for permission by contacting the Hesquiaht First Nation Band Office.

⌘ Estevan Lighthouse – mile 15
Estevan Point Lighthouse is distinctive with its buttressed architecture supporting it against the occasional hurricane force winter winds. Winter storms have been responsible for more damage than the Japanese bombardment on the evening of June 20, 1942. No one was prepared for an attack on the lighthouse when a submarine surfaced in the darkness and fired more than twenty rounds at the station. Without injury or any substantial damage, Estevan Point still goes down in history as the only attack on Canadian soil since 1812.

⌇⤢◆ Hesquiat Village – mile 20
On the southeast shore of Hesquiat Peninsula, the First Nations settlement of Hesquiat is all but abandoned with one or two families occupying a couple of the remaining houses.

⌂ Hesquiat Harbour – mile 21
It is 3 miles of open water from Matlahaw Point across the shallow and often treacherous waters of Hesquiat Bar to Hesquiat Point. Depending on the swell height and direction, a few miles of paddling into Hesquiat Harbour is worth it for the wonderful beaches inside Antons Spit.

⌘ Cougar Annie's Garden – mile 25
In 1915, a spirited pioneer women arrived in Hesquiat Harbour and homesteaded in the wilderness. Tales of wild animals, rifles and rugged individualism earned her the name Cougar Annie. Annie gave birth to 8 children at Hesquiat and outlived 4 husbands. Her legacy is a wonderful garden carved out of 2 hectares of dense rainforest. Abandoned for many years, the garden now has a caretaker and tours can be arranged. The book *Cougar Annie's Garden* by Margaret Horsfield, brings much truth to the more fanciful fiction.

⌘ Hooksum Outdoor Leadership Training Centre
Across from Cougar Annie's you may see a rustic kitchen structure and a fine longhouse above the beach near Rae Basin. Karen and Steve Charleson operate Hooksum Outdoor Leadership Training Centre from this site within the park.

Cedar canoes

Western Red Cedars are found along the entire west coast of Vancouver Island. Reaching 75 m (250 ft) tall and 5.5 m (18 ft) in diameter they have been known to live 1,500 years. Cedar contains unusually high levels of tannins, aromatic oils and resins that inhibit growth of fungi and bacteria, making the wood rot resistant.

For the Nuu-chah-nulth people who have inhabited Vancouver Island's west coast for more than 5,000 years, cedar was a principle source of material for crafts and construction. In spring, women collected cedar bark. Making a horizontal cut in the bark, they slowly pulled upward and outward until the bark came free of the tree. Never stripping more than a third of its circumference, the tree would heal leaving a distinctive scar. The soft, pliable inner bark was separated from the brittle outer bark then hung to dry. The dried bark was split and trimmed for making baskets, cradles, cordage and mats.

Young men learned how to split planks off standing trees, with a technique that kept the trees alive. Planks were used for many purposes, including containers, house siding and roofing. Cedar was used to make house posts and totem poles. Buoyant and rot-resistant, cedar is excellent for making canoes.

The Nuu-chah-nulth, who were the only whale hunters on Canada's Pacific coast, travelled the full length of Vancouver Island and as much as 30 miles offshore in carved cedar dugout canoes to hunt whales. Their canoes were the pride and wealth of the native people and the abundance of cedar trees along the west coast made canoe construction possible.

Canoes designs followed traditional forms based on function and marine conditions, varying in size for use by one person or large enough for thirty people. The Nuu-chah-nulth canoe design is elegant, seaworthy and fast. The flared sides, and raised stern gave stability on rough seas and a flat bottom aided launching, landing and loading at beaches.

Hewn from giant cedars, whaling canoes seldom exceeded 12 metres in length, but large freighter canoes were 15 to 20 metres-long. After carefully felling the chosen tree, they cut away the excess wood then dragged the partially-formed canoe to the water and floated it back to their village. Once the sides and bottom were thinned to the proper dimensions, the canoe was soaked and steamed so the sides could be stretched to the canoe's full width. The sides were held apart by the thwarts, and seat boards. Separately carved bow and stern pieces added distinction to the canoe. Nuu-chah-nulth legends tells that when the Sea-Wolf is in trouble the killer whale will come to his rescue. Honor is given to the legend by decorating the distinctive long prow with an effigy of the head of a wolf.

For the Nuu-chah-nulth the canoe had utilitarian and spiritual values. The living cedar tree sustained a vast community of plants, insects and animals. Felled and transformation into a magnificent ocean-going canoe, the great cedar began a new life in support of the human community.

Openit Inlet and village from the air. Hot Springs Cove in the top right.

Maquinna Provincial Marine Park

Maquinna Provincial Marine Park continues from Hesquiat Provincial Park and covers most of the east coast of Hesquiat Harbour from Rae Basin to Sharp Point. The park includes the hot mineral springs of Hot Springs Cove in Openit Inlet. Camping is permitted throughout the park except near the hot springs. The Hesquiat First Nation operates a campground near the hot springs, north of the government dock. There is also a small store on the reserve on the west shore of Openit Inlet.

⌘✗〰 Hot Springs Cove – mile 28

Several times each day water taxis and float planes transport tourists from Tofino to Hot Springs Cove. From the dock it is 30 minutes along a boardwalk through rainforest to the pungent smell of sulphur hot baths where the hot spring-water tumbles down rocks into half a dozen small pools.

There is considerable boat traffic in and out of the inlet and great care must be taken when fog reduces visibility.

⌂✗◆ Hot Springs Village – mile 29

this small village is located on the west side of Hot Springs Cove and is home to the Hesquiat First Nation. Facilities include a small store, gas dock and camping area.

Clayoquot Sound from the air on a calm day with low swell breaking on the rocks.

☒ Sharp Point – mile 28

At Sharp Point the outgoing ebb current from Sydney Inlet encounters incoming westerly winds creating locally rough sea conditions.

From Openit Inlet there is a choice of travelling inside or outside of Flores Island. The inside route follows the sheltered waters of Sydney Inlet, Shelter Inlet and Millar Channel.

⌂ Sulphur Passage Provincial Park – mile 38

This park is adjacent to the northeast corner of Flores Island and comprises Obstruction Island, Sulphur Passage and the north shore of Shelter Inlet. Random wilderness camping is allowed. The quiet waters of this west coast fjord are surrounded by old-growth Sitka spruce forests and contain a ecologically sensitive estuary. Fifty hectares at the mouth of the Megin River is an ecological reserve. The reserve is open for nature observation and photography but camping is not permitted.

⌂ Sydney Inlet Provincial Park – mile 35

lies north of Flores Island and is one of the most dramatic fjords on Vancouver Island. The park protects old-growth forests and portions of the Sydney River estuary. Camping is permitted but the very steep shoreline provides only limited access.

⌂ Flores Island Provincial Park

the park occupies the western and southern parts of Flores Island and has one of the highest concentrations of Nuu-chah-nulth heritage sites in Clayoquot Sound. Gray whales pass by on their northbound migration and occasionally stop to feed in Cow Bay, making Flores Island one of the most popular destinations in Clayoquot Sound.

⌂ Halfmoon Beach – mile 29

in Sydney Channel east of Sharp Point, Halfmoon Beach provides camping before choosing the inside or the outside routes around Flores Island.

The outside of Flores Island south from Halfmoon Beach is 8 miles of exposed wave swept shore. Past Rafel Point, Siwash Cove is rugged with few or no safe landing sites before Ahous Bay.

Originally used by the Nuu-chah-nulth First Nations, the "Walk the Wild Side Trail", extends 10 km from the village of Ahousaht to the top of Mount Flores. There is also a trail 32 km around the island following sandy beaches and crossing the headlands with some boardwalk sections.

Random wilderness camping is allowed.

⊠ Rafael Point – mile 32

is a prominent headland with a shallow rocky shoreline. Seas can be windswept and rough on most afternoons.

⊠⌂ Cow Bay – mile 36

is exposed to swell and surf is common.

In recent years eco-tourism tours and education programs have done much to aid in the preservation of coastal eco-systems.

Friendly Cove to Tofino & Clayoquot Sound – 129

Tofino from the air.

⌂ Gibson Provincial Marine Park – Whitesand Cove – mile 51

is located on the south side of Flores Island, adjacent to the provincial park and immediately south of the Nuu-chah-nulth community of Ahousaht. There is a trail leading from the beach to Matilda Inlet where a natural warm spring flows into an open concrete tank.

Vargas Island

Close to Tofino, Vargas Island is a very popular kayaking destination. The park includes the western portion of Vargas Island and Blunden Island. Much of Vargas is flat and contains a number of bogs. The west shore of the island is an exposed a rocky coast interrupted by sandy beaches.

The northern and eastern shores are more sheltered channels with many small bays. On their way to northern waters, Gray whales will sometime linger in the area around Ahous Bay. From Ahous Beach there is a 3-km trail that crosses the island from east to west. The neighbouring Cleland Island Ecological Reserve protects sea bird colonies and all access to the reserve is prohibited.

⌘ Vargas Island Lodge

With all the comfort of home, this lodge is a popular with sea kayak outfitters as a base camp or a premier stopover. Located in a small bay half a mile north of Moses Point, the lodge is nestled in the trees above the beach. A stay includes comfortable lodge-based accommodation and great meals; including wild salmon barbeques.

⌂ Ahous Bay – mile 45

Ahous Bay is by far the largest beach on Vargas Island. An estuary in the middle of the bay is surrounded by large sand dunes and leads back into the low and boggy sections of the island. The surf is largest in the middle of the beach with easier access behind rocky outcrops at either end. The end of the beach nearest Ahous Point provides easier landings and the most protection from steady winds.

⊠ Ahous Point – mile 46

Ahous Point is prominent and shallow. Sea conditions off the point are often rough in the afternoon.

⌂ Milties Beach – mile 45

Milties Beach is located on the northern shore of Vargas Island along Calmus Passage and was once a homestead. Partially sheltered yet with a western exposure more like the open coast, it can be subject to some surf. With its good exposure and reasonable shelter it is a very popular camping area and you are unlikely to be alone.

⌘ Epper Passage Provincial Park

The park includes the Dunlap and Morfee islands which lie between Meares and Vargas islands in Calmus Passage. Rocky shores and steep terrain make the park unsuitable for camping. However, a paddle among the islands offers a rewarding experience. Fog can arrive quickly and great care must be taken in the narrows

channels that are busy with commercial boat traffic.

Rassier Point – mile 48

Although not part of the park, the several beaches in the vicinity of Rassier Point are popular spots for paddlers stopping for lunch or camping. Some of the beaches look inviting but upon closer inspection the high tide line rises close to the trees. Choose your campsite carefully, especially when the moon is full or new and the tides are at their highest.

Meares Island

Meares Island is a part of the Tla-O-Qui-Aht and Ahousaht First Nations land that has been declared a Tribal Park and camping is permitted on some areas of the island. The shallow and narrow channels of Browning Passage to the south of Meares and Matlset Narrows to the north can run in excess of 4 knots. Without specific current reference stations in the tide tables a little local knowledge is very useful. To further complicate the narrow passages there is considerable marine traffic in the vicinity of Tofino.

Straight across from Tofino the trailhead to the popular Big Tree Trail is located across from Morpheus Island. The 3-km loop trail is wet and the boardwalks over boggy sections can be very slippery.

As you travel counterclockwise around Meares there is camping at the head of Windy Bay. The bay is well situated to funnel the wind, but at least the mosquitoes are kept away. Once through Dawley Pass there is camping in Heelboom Bay; note that the substantial ebb current flows unexpectedly to the north through Dawley Pass. Mosquito Harbour does not have the wind to keep the bugs away but you can camp near Sutton Mill Creek. A trail leads from Mosquito Harbour up to the largest cedar on the island; 6 metres in diameter. The northern shore of Meares is steep with no opportunity to camp until Ritchie Bay. While paddling around Meares Island, pay close attention to the highest tides that leave little or no beach exposed. Look for campsites among the trees above the beach.

For more information on Meares Island Tribal Park contact the Nuuchah-nulth Info Centre in Tofino.

⌘▢♨↗◆ Tofino – mile 50

Tofino is a growing community of 1,500 with over a million tourists visiting each year. Centrally located in the Clayoquot Sound and adjacent to Pacific Rim National Park, the community is blessed with spectacular natural beauty. Despite its small size, the village centre and surrounding commercial and residential area offers a remarkable variety of services. Accommodations of all kinds are very busy during summer and reservations are strongly recommended.

Short excursions

Clayoquot Sound

Sea kayaking in Clayoquot Sound is a well-established recreational activity. Depending on your skill level and interest you can plan your own trip or join one of the many sea kayak outfitters that operate out of Tofino. Tofino's location is ideal for taking guided daytrips and multi-day excursions to the close-at-hand marine wilderness. Tofino Sea Kayaking Company, located at 320 Main Street, is a good place to pick up local information.

In addition to the boat ramp at the foot of 1st Street, there is a launch site at Grice Bay within Pacific Rim National Park. Turn off Highway 4 on Grice Bay Road. Park user fees and regulations apply. Inquire at the park information centre or at Green Point Campground both on highway 4.

The inside waters of Clayoquot Sound are complex waterways with locally strong currents, frequent fog and a good deal of boat traffic. Beginners need to be guided by a leader with good local knowledge. Intermediate paddlers should research all necessary tide and weather information before venturing out on their own.

- Easily accessible day trips include paddles to Meares, Stubbs, Wickaninnish and Vargas islands.
- The east coast of Vargas Island is a one-hour paddle north from Tofino. Once ashore on the gentle east coast, the magnificence of Ahous Beach and the other exposed beaches of the west coast are accessible via trails leading across the island.
- The Vargas Island Lodge offers deluxe sea kayak lodge based adventures. You will need to contact a sea kayak outfitter to book a stay at the lodge.
- A circumnavigation of Meares Island takes the paddler through a sheltered wilderness without exposure to long expanses of open water.

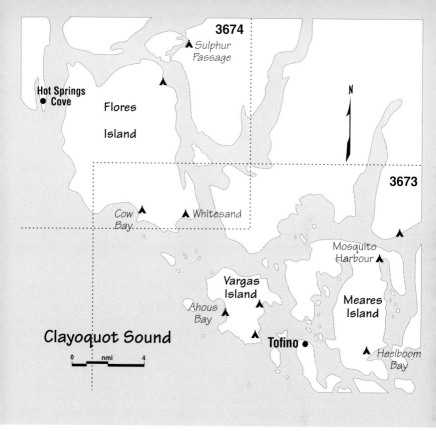

Clayoquot Sound

There are areas of fast moving tidal current in the narrow channels. Appropriate local knowledge and the use of tide tables can make for an exciting and safe trip.

- Water taxi service is available to almost any nearby destination including more remote locations such as Sulphur Passage Provincial Park behind Flores Island.

- Tofino is also a popular location for improving one's paddling skills. Local sea kayak outfitters offer courses which include surf skills, seamanship and navigation necessary for longer self-sufficient trips.

8

Tofino to Port Renfrew & Barkley Sound

Distance 80 nmi
Duration 6 travelling days
Charts #3671, #3670, #3673 #3602, #3603, #3606
>   Chart coverage for this region is quite mixed with some areas poorly
>   covered by 1:150 000 scale charts. The Broken Group Islands is cov-
>   ered by a special collectors edition 1:20 000 scale chart that includes
>   campsite information and additional wildlife information on the back.

Tides and Current Tables Vol. 6
Tide Reference Stations Tofino
Current Reference Stations not applicable
Weather Broadcast Region West Coast Vancouver Island South
Weather Reporting Stations La Perouse, Tofino, Leonard Island, Amphirite
Island, Cape Beale, Pachena, Carmanah
Coast Guard Services Tofino, Bamfield

Pacific Rim National Park dominates this section of coastline, and visitors from around the world come to walk the trails, surf the fine sandy beaches and watch winter storms hurl Pacific swells onto shore. The park consists of three separate geographical areas: Long Beach, the Broken Group Islands and the West Coast Trail. Features include sand beaches, an island archipelago, old-growth coastal temperate rainforest and significant archaeological sites.

Numerous archaeological sites have been identified within the park. The diverse and coastal ecology provided abundant food, clothing and shelter, leaving time for natives to develop sophisticated art and culture. Within the complex native culture, all the animals of the air, land and sea were spiritually significant. The western red cedar was a primary resource and a cultural centerpiece. The bark was used for weaving clothing, blankets, and containers. The supple rot-resistant timber was ideal for building houses and canoes. The sea provided abundant fish, seal, sea lions, and whales for food and other materials. At the time of first European contact, the region was estimated to have a population of over 9,000. Unfortunately, the introduction of firearms, alcohol and infectious diseases by foreign traders devestated native communities. In less than 100 years, internal warfare and disease had decimated the population and contributed to the complete disruption of some culturally distinct subgroups.

Once a remote fishing village Tofino is now a thriving tourist centre with

It was difficult to avoid numerous grey whales lounging near the mouth of the Klanawah River.

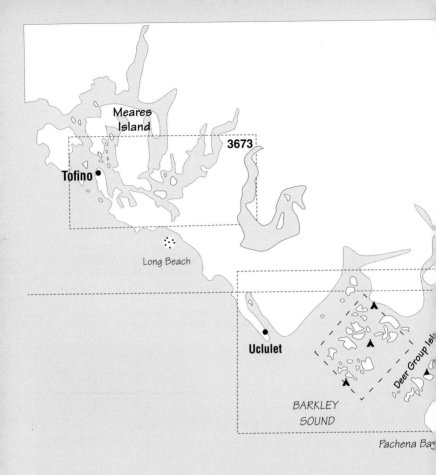

Meares
Island

3673

Tofino

Long Beach

 Uclulet

BARKLEY
SOUND

Deer Group Isl

Pachena Bay

0   nmi   5

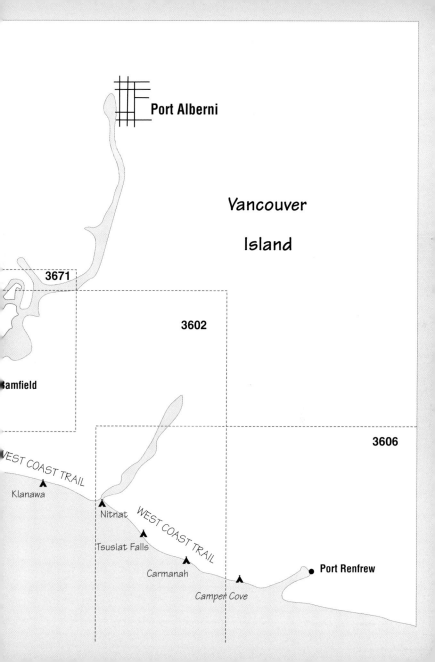

The West Coast Trail

Along the shore from Cape Beale to Port Renfrew impressive sandstone cliffs weathered into caves and sea arches, are interrupted by shallow surf-swept beaches. Pacific storms and strong oceanic currents cast many vessels onto the rocks and shoals of this rugged coast. Since 1803, over 240 ships have foundered along this shore. Sailors who survived and made it to shore found no refuge and often perished in the impassible rainforest. In 1874 a lighthouse was built at Cape Beale to warn ships away from the dangers of this coast. Further improvements to the region were completed in 1890 and included a rough trail and telegraph line between Victoria and Cape Beale and a second lighthouse at Carmanah Point.

On January 20, 1906 the Valencia, a 253 ft iron steamer left San Francisco bound for Victoria. Two days later, in the dead of night her Captain ran the Valencia aground at Pachena Point. Only 30 meters from land, the Valencia, launched her lifeboats into the violent surf. None of the 6 lifeboats reached shore. Construction of a third lighthouse began the following year near the wreck site. Improvements were made to the rough trail between Bamfield and Carmanah Point. The improved trail included simple cabins to shelter the few shipwreck victims who were able to make it to shore. Unfortunately, the cost of improving the trail became excessive and the trail remained unimproved beyond Carmanah. Shipwrecks continued to occur with regularity, and this length of coast deservedly earned the reputation of being "the Graveyard of the Pacific".

As the accuracy of navigation and the reliability of engines improved, the number of wrecks declined and the trail ceased to be regularly maintained. The original rough trail quickly became overgrown and impassible. In 1973, the long abandoned trail was resurrected as a recreational trail and became part of included in Pacific Rim National Park.

Photo: Gillean Daffern.

camping, whale watching and kayak adventure businesses. Most camping areas along the shore from Tofino south to the Port San Juan are either administered by the park service or are privately owned. Random wilderness camping is very limited so plan ahead. There are a number of commercial campgrounds accessible to kayaks in the Tofino area including Bella Pacifica campground and Crystal Cove Resort in the Mackenzie Beach area. For the more refined kayaker there are several recreational resorts with waterfront cabins. On a long trip down the coast, you can make use of these facilities, stopping to clean up and re-supply before moving on to the next tentsite under the stars.

The Broken Group Islands in Barkley Sound are a world-renowned sea kayak destination. The outer reaches of the sound are fully exposed to west coast swell and wind, but most of the closely packed archipelago provides abundant shelter from all but the worst weather systems. Sandy coves, shallow lagoons and complex shorelines make paddling in the Broken Group Island accessible to most paddlers. Designated campsites are busy in mid summer.

Paddling Conditions
Beginners have many opportunities to be guided through Clayoquot and Barkley sounds.

Intermediate paddlers can paddle anywhere in the two sounds, although if they are travelling the outer coast, should seek the assistance of advanced paddlers familiar with the area.

Advanced paddlers should plan landing sites in careful consideration with the swell and wind forecast. Advanced paddling skills are required for the West Coast Trail from Cape Beale to Port San Juan. Steep gravel beaches have surf that can be steep and plunging close to shore. Some sections of the coast have shallow sandstone shelves making access to shore difficult. During the summer months, the west entrance to the Strait of Juan de Fuca is subject to strong west winds in the afternoon.

Safety considerations
VHF radio communications are good in the area with Canada Coast Guard stations in Tofino and Bamfield. Cell phone reception is improving near some populated centres. High-speed boat traffic is a significant hazard during times of fog and I would advise crossing open passages when visability is good. If you must travel across open water with limited visibility, announce your intention on VHF Channel 16 and monitor the radio at all times.

Along the open coast, a combination of long surf-swept beaches and rocky shores with sandstone shelves backed with high cliffs, provides few landing opportunities. Waiting for good swell conditions and good planning are strongly advised.

Marine traffic
Ucluelet and Bamfield are popular for sport fishing all year round and the area is particularly busy during the September Labour Day weekend fishing derby. There is also a considerable

Visibility reduced to near zero in fog

In the dense fog I can see only one whale at a time, but I can hear the metallic ring of several others exhaling around me. They are snoozing near the surface, drifting in small circles just outside of the line of breakers, breathing rhythmically every 30 seconds. Without sight of the shore I measure the rise and fall of the swell as it echoes the shallow bottom and lifts perceptibly; this is literally navigation by the seat of the pants.

The fog thins and I can see whales ahead, Tsusiat Falls to my left and an abandoned 16 ft. run-about powerboat to my right. Nobody answers my calls. The fog closes in again and it is just me, the abandoned boat, and the sound of whales and surf. My arms keep moving and the paddle pulls me forward past Nitnat bar with its infamous boat-eating surf and then the extended reefs of Bonilla Point. The occasional cresting wave and the ever-present thunder of surf guide me along the fringe of the breakers. Following this line, my watch and my compass tell me I am turning into Carmanah Bay and surf landing in the fog.

It's eerie and tense. The monochrome universe of thick fog and calm sea challenges ones belief in every decision. North becomes south, near becomes far and sooner becomes later. At the limit of visibility I can see the swell running parallel along low cliffs and breaking on jagged outcrops of rock. Creeping one paddle stroke at a time and occasionally back paddling, the heaving swell slips beneath me as the water becomes shallow and the face of the waves becomes steep. The increasing slope on the swell is my only measure of distance from the invisible shore. I take my last chance to pause, clear the deck and snug my life jacket. Waves are breaking to my left, to my right and dead ahead and growing steeper as they pass beneath me. I am questioning my compass, my hearing, and my navigation. The next wave rises up, cresting, threatening to break. My kayak points downhill, accelerating, lifting up out of the water surfing the face. I am committed and dig the paddle in deep, pulling forward into a high-speed charge for the safety or calamity of the shore. My head snaps back with sensory whiplash as my monochrome world explodes into full sun and colour. My wave of death stretches out flat and I glide into a gently undulating kelp bed fringing a wide arc of white sand.

A harbour seal leaps into the air reentering the water, slapping his tail with a sharp report. To the right a rainbow arches over the trees and on the left Carmanah Lighthouse reaches into a clear sky. On the beach beneath the lighthouse there is a lean-to built of driftwood with smoke spiraling out through the blue-tarp roof.

Arriving on the beach I drag my kayak up the sand to a likely tent site amongst the logs. Cold wet clothes are traded for dry shorts before walking over to the lean-to. The sand is too hot for bare feet I have to double back for sandals. Under the tarp, amid rising smoke there is a lady standing behind an enormous wood-burning stove and two fellows sitting on a makeshift bench eating burgers. Just a couple of minutes ago I was in a cold grey spherical world, riding the cresting wave-of-death and now I am sitting down with two hikers from Germany and a French speaking Algonquin Indian who operates a lean-to beachfront driftwood bistro. "Two beer and a double cheeseburger please."

volume of high-speed traffic of water taxis and whale-watching boats. The Francis Barkley and the Lady Rose run scheduled freight and passenger service between Ucluelet, Bamfield, throughout Barkley Sound and to Port Alberni.

Large ocean-going ships and barges occasionally sail from the industrial facilities in Port Alberni through Imperial Eagle Channel.

Principle points of access

Both Tofino (to the north) and Port Renfrew (to the south) are at the terminus of highways. From Victoria or Nanaimo there is access to Tofino and Ucluelet along Highway 4. Summer accommodation in Tofino is much sought after, be sure you have made arrangements in advance.

Port Renfrew can be reached by driving 90 km along Highway 14 from Victoria. Port Renfrew is a small village with few amenities, but you should be able to find what you need.

Coastal trip

Tofino mile 0

Refer to Section 7 for information about Tofino.

⌂⌇⌂ Bella Pacifica Campground – mile 1.5

A simple clean and accessible private campground with hot showers, laundry facilities and pay phones; open from February to October. Advance reservations are required for summer camping.

⌘⌂⌂ Cox Bay – mile 4

Cox Bay is a good surfing beach with a commercial campground behind the beach.

⌘⌂ Long Beach – mile 9

Long Beach is a central feature of Pacific Rim National Park and is usually busy with swimmers, surfers, sunbathers and a general swarm of tourists. There is no camping along the beach. Green Point Campground, south of Long Beach, is high above the beach on a cliff and not easily reached by kayakers. If you are thinking about stopping at Green Point for a couple of nights you will need to make reservations well in advance. However, about a dozen or so walk-in campsites are available on a first come first served basis; if you arrive mid-week and before lunch you may just find a spot.

There is pay parking throughout Pacific Rim Park. Day and seasons passes are available.

⌂⌇⌂◆ Ucluelet – mile 21

Ucluelet (pronounced yoo-CLOO-let) is a small town of about 2,000 located on the northern edge of Barkley Sound and is the western terminus for the Lady Rose and the Francis Barkley.

From Amphirite Point across Loudou channel to the southwest reaches of the Broken Group Islands is 7 miles of open water. You are better off to depart Ucluelet early in the day and avoid often strong afternoon onshore winds.

⊠ Benson Island – mile 28

After crossing Loudou Channel, the first of the Broken Group Islands within Pacific Rim Park is Benson Island. The island's outer shores are swept by Pacific swell but there is a lovely sheltered channel between Benson and Clarke islands. There is excellent camping on or above the beach on the northeast part of the island. The island was named after John Benson, who operated a hotel there for several decades.

⊠ Clarke Island – mile 28

Adjacent to Benson Island, the north shore of Clarke Island offers additional fine campsites on a sandy beach. Before they were hunted to near extinction two hundred years ago, sea otters inhabited the shores of Drum Rocks and Pigot Islets east of Clarke and Benson Island. In recent years, sea otters have been seen in Clayoquot Sound just 30 miles to the north. Since their reintroduction in the Bunsby Islands, Sea Otters are increasing in numer and the otter population is now approaching Barkley Sound.

Farther northeast into the Broken Group there are more designated camping areas on Turret, Willis, Dodd Gibraltar and Gilbert islands. (Refer to short excursions page 146).

Wouwer, Howell and Cree Islands delineate the outer edge of the Broken Group Islands. Rugged and beautiful, the southwestern shores are awash with swell breaking over numerous rock outcrops. California, and occasionally Steller sea lions, will haul-out on the rocks and islet near Wouwer Island. On a calm day it is possible to land on these outer is-

lands. The large intertidal area on the southwest side of Wouwer Island is a good spot to beachcoam and inspect tide pools. As you pass Cree Island you exit the park and have 3.5 nmi of open water to cross before reaching Folger Island, the outermost island of the Deer Group.

⌘ Dodger Channel – mile 36

Dodger Channel runs between Edward King and Diana islands, and is so named because sailors frequently used it to 'dodge in' out of bad weather. In 1901, Captain John Voss departed Victoria in a 38 foot canoe bound for an around-the-world voyage. In his first days he dodged a gale by entering the shelter of Dodger Channel. He was so impressed by the scenery and local people that he lingered a month before setting out across the Pacific (see Venturesome Voyages of Captain Voss).

⤢⚓◆ Bamfield – mile 39

This hamlet of 200 located in a protected inlet on the south shore of Barkley Sound, boasts a variety of restaurants, galleries, shops, equipment rentals and accommodations. Bamfield is divided in two parts, separated by about 200 metres of Bamfield Inlet. Bamfield-west has a waterfront boardwalk connecting homes, docks and a few small businesses. Most businesses, including a pub, market and café are in Bamfield-east.

⊠ Cape Beale – mile 43

Cape Beale is the rugged southwesterly entrance to Barkley Sound. Good weather and sea conditions are necessary when rounding this cape. Tidal

Bamfield Cable Station

In 1846 W. E. Banfield, a ships carpenter, arrived in Barkley Sound aboard HMS Constance. Many years later the tiny settlement where he came ashore to live was named Banfield Creek. Following the coastal survey of 1932 the village fell victim to a postal error: the postmaster misspelled the name as Bamfield, exchanging the n for an m. With the tenacity of a barnacle adhering to a rock, the new spelling took hold and remains today. The village came out of obscurity in 1902 when Bamfield was chosen as the eastern terminus of the trans-Pacific telegraph cable. A relay station was constructed and the cable was laid 4,000 miles across the Pacific to Fanning Island, a tiny coral atoll in the mid-Pacific. From there the cable continued onto Fiji, New Zealand and Australia. The Bamfield cable station served as a relay point on the end of a segment of an around the world submarine cable telegraph system. The facilities in Bamfield Inlet consisted of a powerhouse, offices, a superintendent's residence, a bunkhouse for single men and bungalows for married couples. Administered by a head office in Sydney Australia, most of the 45 staff in Bamfield were Australians and New Zealanders.

The tiny station was critical to the efforts of both World Wars. During WWI the Italians cut the Mediterranean cables, so all communications between North Africa and London had to be sent via cables through the Indian Ocean to Australia, on to Bamfield, relayed across North America on land lines and then finally relayed again by submarine cable across the Atlantic to Britain. The cable was doubled in 1926 and a new three-storey building was erected on the hillside below the earlier buildings. The federal government kept a close eye on this international communication link. On June 20, 1942 when enemy submarines fired shells onto Vancouver Island near Estevan Lighthouse just 20 mile to the north, security at the cable station was given prime importance. It was heavily guarded with fences, barbed wire, artillery and military personnel.

Improvements in technology led to automation of cable services, and in 1956 the staff was reduced to just 5 maintenance personnel. The last message was relayed in June 1959. The cable station changed hands in 1969 when a consortium of 5 western Canadian Universities purchased the property and redeveloped it into Bamfield Marine Biological Station. The research facility now houses academic staff and students. The first road reached Bamfield in late 1963.

currents flowing out of the Sound meet incoming swell and wind waves making for difficult sea conditions. Several shallow reefs offshore create large isolated boomers.

Once rounding Cape Beale you are travelling along the superbly rugged and challenging shoreline of the West Coast Trail. Depending on the swell size and direction you may find a few small sandy coves; but more often than not the beaches are of steep gravel or shelving rock. Landings through short plunging surf should be anticipated.

Stellar sea lions on rock with Carmanah Lighthouse in the background.

⌂≈✈ Pachena Bay – mile 46

Pachena Bay reaches well into the shoreline and can be protected from much of the ocean swell. There is wilderness camping on the open beach or nearby, in the Pachena Bay Campground (operated by the Huu-ay-aht (Ohiaht) First Nation in Bamfield). The campground has hot showers, flush toilets, a store and other services.

⌂≈ Klanawah River – mile 53

Klanawah River is one of many spots you can stop, but typical of this stretch of coastline it has a steep gravel beach accessible only in low swell conditions. The river may not be visible from seaward as large gravel berms sometimes block the river mouth entirely creating a fine swimming hole behind the berm. Above the beach is an interesting hand-powered cable tram which transports hikers over the river.

⌂≈ Tsusiat Falls – mile 55

The falls are an ongoing attraction and the beach is flatter than most. Once through the surf, you are likely to find many hikers camped for a day or more. The popularity of camping at Tsusiat Falls can be a distraction from its wild beauty. You may choose to stop at Tsusiat Falls for a break and move on to overnight at another spot.

⌂ Tsusiat Point (Hole in the Wall)

East of the falls there is a wonderful stone arch and less busy camping on the nearby beach.

⊠ Nitnat River Bar – mile 58

The shallow bar is notorious for its rough surf and strong currents. It is best to give it a wide berth in all but the very best conditions.

⌘ Clo-oose – mile 60

There is a lovely sand beach at Clo-oose. In the early 1900's, the West Coast Development Company had great plans to build a hotel, golf courses and large family houses on the seashore. They distributed masses of literature to attract would-be buyers and eventually a nucleus of 40 or 50 people were attracted to the west coast wilderness around Clo-oose. Although illusions of grand land development were rekindled after WWI and the population of hopeful investors rose to two hundred, they eventually abandoned the site.

△ Carmanah – mile 63

A spectacular long beach extends west from the magnificent lighthouse on the point. If the summer swell is from the northwest you will have an easy landing near the lighthouse. Here you will share the beach, and likely a few stories, with hikers from the West Coast Trail.

⊠△ Bonilla Point – mile 66

The shelving rock and rocky shallows that make Bonilla Point a marine hazard also provide a section of flat sandy beach good for camping. Within the trees, a creek falls to the beach just right for a welcome shower.

△↗ Camper Cove – mile 72.5

Camper Cove is a busy spot for hikers and one of the few places along the West Coast Trail that is accessible by powerboat. It serves as an evacuation point and there is a trail guardian's cabin located here.

Owen Point – mile 74

Seas can be confused around Owen Point. There is a shallow reef close to shore which you can either go around or paddle inside the reef very close to shore. Port San Juan faces the open Pacific, and on occasions when the swell direction lines up with the bay the waves can be enormous one day and near flat the next. The beach drops abruptly into deep water and the surf plunges very near shore. When the swell runs high caution is strongly advised near shore. On warm summer days the valley at the head of Port San Juan heats up and the rising air creates a strong in-flow wind. There can be calm air on the coast and 20 knots of wind at the head of bay.

△ Thrasher Cove mile – mile 75.5

Thrasher Cove lies in the partial shelter of Port San Juan. It is the last stop before the hamlet of Port Renfrew and the small campsite is often crowded with hikers during peak season.

△〰 Gordon River – mile 78

If waves are breaking on the long beach, you can access the shore at the west end of the beach a short distance up the Gordon River. Campsites accessible by kayaks are found at the Pacheedaht First Nations campground on the beach at the river mouth or the Port Renfrew Marina & R.V. Park a short distance up river in a narrow backwater (open May to October).

⚐⚓ San Juan River – mile 79.5

At the east end of the beach, the San Juan River also has easy landing and beach access to private camping.

⚐≈⚓ Port Renfrew – mile 80

Port Renfrew at the end of highway is a small village with a growing number of services catering to West Coast Trail hikers and sport fishers.

Short excursions

Barkley Sound

Barkley Sound lies northeast of Ucluelet and SW of Bamfield. The Sound is an area of approximately 800 square kilometres and includes hundreds of small islands in the Broken Group and the Deer Group islands. The popularity of these islands with paddlers has increased dramatically over the past two decades. Barkley Sound is normally sheltered from the harshest weather. Sea kayakers can reach the Broken Group Islands from Port Alberni and Ucluelet onboard either the MV Lady Rose or the MV Frances Barkley.

The Nuu-chah-nulth people once occupied large villages in the Broken Group and Deer Group Islands. Prior to contact with Europeans, the native population of Barkley Sound is estimated to have been between 3000 and 5000; village sites, middens, fish traps, culturally modified trees, lookouts and fallen longhouses remain as part of this rich cultural heritage. Archeological sites include stonewall fish traps, shell middens and terraced village sites. Visitors should not disturb any of these sites, and it is illegal to dig in a midden without a permit. The Sound was explored and named in 1787 by Captain Charles William Barkley of the British Trading vessel the Imperial Eagle.

Wildlife on the islands includes minks, martens, river otters and

Looking north from Dicebox Island into the Broken Group Islands.

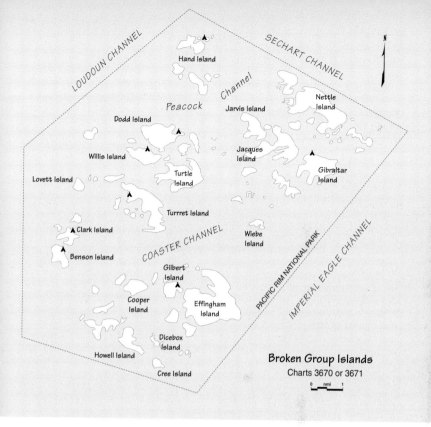

Broken Group Islands
Charts 3670 or 3671

0 nmi 1

raccoons. Columbian black-tailed deer inhabit the forested islands, and hundreds of seabirds nest in the sound. There is abundant bird life during spring and fall migration, as flocks stop to rest and feed. Barkley Sound has a thriving population of bald eagles many of which nest high in the evergreen trees. Marine life includes killer whales and grey whales, porpoises, basking sharks, harbour seals and California and Steller's sea lions.

Paddling conditions
In summer Barkley Sound is normally sheltered from the winds and swell found on the exposed west coast. Winter in Barkley Sound can produce heavy rain, fog, rough seas, swells and heavy weather. The best paddling is from April to October, and the peak season for visitors is July and August.

Beginners under the leadership of a guide or an intermediate paddler with local knowledge will find the region to be a safe adventure.

Baleen Whales

Baleen whales have large jaws that open wide to scoop huge volumes of food. The jaw is fringed with comb-like baleen that filters out food when the water is expelled. Baleen whales typically seen along the Vancouver Island coast are Grey, Humpback, and Minke.

The annual 10,000-mile migration of the grey whale from southern California to Alaska is an outstanding natural event. Most individuals pass within a mile from shore, providing a popular whale-watching spectacle. On occasion, grey whales will enter shallow bays to rest and feed, sometimes for several weeks, before continuing their migration. Unlike the more typical baleen whales, grey whales feed by drawing in soft-bottom sediments and straining out the many shrimps and sea worms found in the muck. Grey whales are recognized by their mottled-grey colour and low bumpy ridge instead of a dorsal fin. Adult whales are 35 to 50 feet long and weigh 15 to 45 tons.

Humpback whales feed on krill and small fish and are similar in size to grey whales. They can be identified by their darker skin, knobby head and short thick dorsal fin placed well back toward the tail (caudal fin). The flippers of a Humpback are lightly coloured and unusually long, up to one-third of their body length. Like gray whales, humpbacks migrate between summer feeding grounds in colder waters and winter breeding grounds in warmer environments. Humpbacks are known for breaching—launching their immense bulk out of the water in tremendous displays of power. While all whales use some form of sound for echolocation, humpbacks males are renowned for hanging vertically head down and 'singing' their eerie whale song at great length.

Minke whales are another species of baleen whale sometimes spotted on the Vancouver Island coast. Much smaller than a grey or humpback, the minke whale has a small dorsal fin located quite far forward on the body. The head is pointed and dark in colour. There is a distinctive white patch on the flippers. As the whale ascends to blow, its dorsal fin is visible immediately its body breaks the surface. They are known to breach clear of the water in an elegant arch. Minke whales feed on fish and krill.

Intermediate paddlers can wander throughout the sound, saving the exposed southwestern shores for calm days with stable weather. The 4 nmi crossing of Imperial Eagle Channel can be subject to swell and the full force of southwesterly winds.

Safety

When summer storms arrive they usually last one to three days and are followed by a period of better weather. During a particularly good July or August, the weather may be fine for two or three weeks at a time. Good weather can bring sea fog that develops as warm air moves over cool water. All areas of open water are subject to swell and westerly wind. Strong afternoon winds can develop, particularly on hot summer days.

Marine Traffic

Sport fishers and ocean-going ships and barges from the pulp and paper mill in Alberni.

There is good radio communication with Bamfield Coast Guard and the Pacific Rim Park wardens who patrol the Broken Group Islands daily.

Access

Passenger & cargo ships MV Lady Rose and MV Francis Barkley operate regular schedules out of Port Alberni. To get to Port Alberni by car from Victoria take highway 1 north, and continue on highway 19 north at Nanaimo. Take Highway 4 west to Port Alberni. Port Alberni is 195 kilometres miles from Victoria. Allow at least 3 hours to get there. The Lady Rose and the Francis Barkley will pick up and drop of kayaks at Sechart within the Broken Group Islands. As an alternative, the Toquart Connector Water Taxi based at Sechart can transport you and your kayaks between Toquart, the Broken Group Islands and Bamfield.

Road access to Bamfield in western Barkley Sound is from Port Alberni. From Port Alberni to Bamfield it is 90 km of well-maintained gravel logging road (approx 1 hr 45 min).

If you are heading to Bamfield from Victoria drive Highway 19 north to Duncan and turn off on Highway 18 to Youbou. Follow the road signs to Bamfield. From Youbou it is a 2 hr 15 min drive on 120 km of logging road. For a good launch site, turn right at the first stop sign in Bamfield and follow Grappler Road to Port Desire.

Another popular access to Barkley Sound is via the Forest Service Rec-

Camp at Hand Island, Broken Group Islands.

reation Site at Toquart Bay. From Port Alberni travel approximately 100 km and turn left onto a gravel road leading in 17 km to Toquart Bay.

Toquart Bay

This site is heavily used by sport fishers and kayakers. The bay is relatively sheltered and provides excellent access to the Broken Islands. It is 5 nmi from Toquart Bay to Hand Island, the nearest campsite in the Broken Group Islands.

Broken Group Island (Pac Rim National Park). Refer to chart #3670.

There are countless islands, islets and rocky outcrops within the Broken Group Islands. Natural features include small lagoons, sandbars, rock formations and secluded coves. Middens, stone fish traps and other archaeological sites remain as evidence of the traditional territory of the Nuu-chah-nulth people. Kayak-accessible designated campsites are available at Hand, Gibraltar, Dodd, Willis, Turret, Benson, Clarke and Gilbert islands. All of these sites are easily reached in less than a day's paddle of one another. Each is clearly marked on the specialty chart #3670. Facilities are limited and drinking water and garbage disposal are not provided. Composting toilets are located at each camp area.

On calm days with stable weather most paddlers can explore the sea caves on the exposed shores of Dempster Island, Dicebox, and Gibraltar Island and Meares Bluff on Effingham Island.

Dear Group Island

The Deer Group Islands are outside of Pacific Rim National Park. It is a 1.5 nmi paddle from Port Desire across the open water of Trevor Channel to the Deer Group Islands. Suitable camping locations and clearings are limited by the dense forest and high tides that rise to the edge of the forest. Although there are good looking camping spots at several Indian reserves, do not land without first obtaining permission from the Huu-ay-aht band office. There is good camping on Diana Island, near the northeast corner and the southern tip. There are a few random wilderness campsites on the east shore of Sanford Island, on the small islets south of Fleming Island, the isthmus on Fleming Island. On northeastern Tzartus Island check out Holford, the adjacent Stud Islets and Sproat Bay to the southeast. Among the Deer Group there are other small coves and islets where you can look for campsites, with best results during neap tides when midnight tides are not too high.

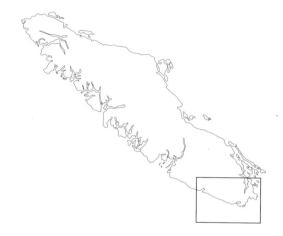

9

Port Renfrew to Victoria & Saanich Inlet

Distance 55 nmi
Duration 4 travelling days
Charts #3606, #3440
Tides and Current Tables Vol. 6
Tide Reference Stations Tofino
Current Reference Stations Race Rocks
Weather Broadcast Region Juan de Fuca Strait
Weather Reporting Stations Sheringham Point, Race Rocks,
    Trial Island, Discovery island, East Point,
Coast Guard Services Victoria, Sooke, Oak Bay

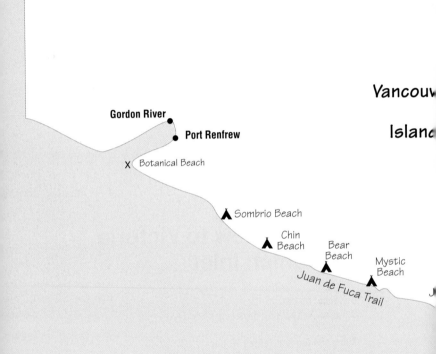

Gordon River

Port Renfrew

X Botanical Beach

Sombrio Beach

Chin
Beach

Bear
Beach

Mystic
Beach

Juan de Fuca Trail

Vancouv

Island

J

0   nmi   5

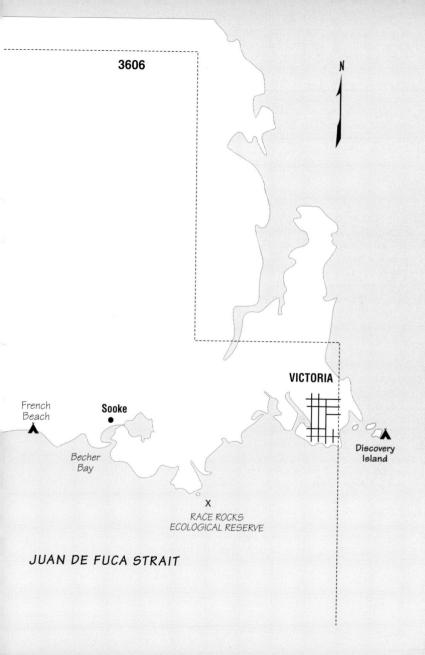

3606

N

VICTORIA

French
Beach

Sooke

Becher
Bay

Discovery
Island

X
RACE ROCKS
ECOLOGICAL RESERVE

JUAN DE FUCA STRAIT

Wind and swell along the Juan de Fuca Strait is moderated by the mountains of the Olympic Peninsula and wind and tide are concentrated in a 10 mile wide corridor created by mountains on both sides of the strait. Marine weather broadcasts issue a small craft warning for the Juan de Fuca Strait every day throughout the summer. Tidal currents run at 2 knots in the middle of the strait and as much as 4 knots close to shallow headlands.

Located at the west entrance to Port San Juan, Botanical Beach has a shelving sandstone shore with tide pools and a fantastic diversity of marine life that has been studied since the early 1900's. Race Rocks to the south has also gained an international reputation as a center for the study of marine life. At the crossroads of the open Pacific and the shelter of the southern Gulf Islands, vigorous tidal currents bring an abundance of nutrients to the water's surface, supporting an eclectic and vibrant marine environment.

Juan de Fuca Trail runs 47 kilometers from Botanical Beach south to the China Beach trailhead. Some of the camping facilities along the trail are on the beach and accessible to kayakers. The shore is steep and rugged with intermittent beaches backed by spruce and cedar forests. The large Sitka spruce trees at Sombrio Beach and China Beach are reminiscent of the mature coastal forest that covered much of Vancouver Island before widespread commercial logging.

Highway 14 parallels the shore from Port Renfrew to Victoria, but the region remains remote and without services until you reach Sooke. Development onshore increases from Sooke to Victoria, and recreational boat traffic becomes very common. Looking well out into the middle of the strait you will see one of the busiest shipping lanes in the world, with freighters, aircraft carriers and cruise ships passing by at all times.

Paddling conditions

This is a coastline without significant bays or inlets and with only infrequent landing sites.

The shoreline is generally rocky with some cliffs and shelving rock punctuated by a variety of sand, gravel and boulder beaches. As you travel east into Juan de Fuca Strait there is increasing shelter from the swell, and surf conditions vary greatly. East of Sombrio River sets of waves can be irregular and vary significantly.

Advanced conditions prevail owing to a lack of shelterd landing sites and persistent winds during times of fair weather. The beaches are exposed, offering little shelter and a generally steep with short plunging surf where ocean swells extend up the strait. Headlands with locally strong tidal currents and rough sea conditions include Point No Point, Beechey Head and Otter Point. Very swift currents occur in the vicinity of Race Rocks where the geography forces the current to change direction.

Beginners can take day trips within the extensive waters inside Sooke Harbour and the interior of Sooke Basin. Under the supervision of an experienced leader, Port San Juan provides excellent opportunities for beginners to train and experience lim-

Shelving sandstone shore typical along the Juan de Fuca shore. Look for intermittent small pocket beaches for easier landing sites.

ited open water conditions. Similar opportunities can be found at Whiffin Spit outside Sooke Harbour.

Intermediate paddlers with surf landing skills can travel the region in times of stable weather. Conditions change dramatically with the arrival of stormy weather. Jordan River, Race Rocks and Trial Island are popular places for intermediate paddlers to train for open coastal conditions; appropriate leadership and local knowledge are absolutely necessary when paddling these areas in moderately rough conditions.

Advanced and intermediate paddlers will travel this region throughout summer and can often be found taking a shake-down trip here in the spring before making longer summer trips on the open west coast.

Safety considerations

The Juan de Fuca Strait is subject to strong westerly afternoon winds during spring and summer. Following a rise in temperature after light easterly winds, westerly winds can abruptly rise to gale force with little visual warning.

From Botanical Beach to China Beach sections of cliffs and shallow rock shelves provide intermittent landing opportunities. Where tidewaters are forced to change direction at Race Rocks and Trial Island, the currents become strong and sea conditions very hazardous, with tide rips running at more than 6 knots.

Sea conditions close to shore at Beechey Head can be rough when ebb tidal streams encounter westerly winds.

Voyage of the Tillicum

John Voss was a deepsea sailor, ships captain and for a time, the proprietor of two hotels in Victoria BC. Captain John Voss was asked by a Canadian journalist named Luxton in 1901 if he could sail around the globe in a vessel smaller than *The Spray*, a 36 foot sloop, in which Joshua Slocum had completed the first solo circumnavigation of the globe in 1898. Voss responded, "I think we can go one better." Looking on the east coast of Vancouver Island for a suitable vessel Voss found an Indian dugout canoe made from a single piece of western red cedar. For a few dollars and a little whiskey he acquired the canoe and outfitted it with a deck, an interior and three small masts. At 38 feet long and with a beam of 5 foot 6 inches, the Tillicum was an unlikely vessel for an around the world cruise.

On May 21, 1901, Voss, with Luxton as crew headed out of the Strait of Juan de Fuca. Poor weather soon forced the canoe into Port San Juan where it waited for seas to calm. Six days later the Tillicum started out across the Pacific. But before noon a gale rose once again and drove them around Cape Beale into the Deer Group Islands. While taking shelter in Dodger Cove, Voss and Luxton found the local natives and the beautiful surroundings so pleasant they remained for a month. Finally they departed for their next port of call in the Marquesas. Three years and several crewmen later Voss ended his 46,000 mile voyage in London, England. While technically Voss' route did not circumnavigate the globe his accomplishment remains undisputed. The Tillicum now rests in the Maritime Museum at Victoria.

Marine traffic

High-speed ferries, pilot boats, naval ships, cruise ships and other commercial vessels travel regularly in and out of Victoria Harbour.

Points of access

Port Renfrew is located two hours from Victoria on highway 14 west of Sooke. Port Renfrew offers good access for kayakers and good camping opportunities. Sooke village has full services, accommodation and a government dock. There is easy access to the water at Cooper Cove east of Sooke and off Whiffin Spit road west of the village.

The Race Rocks area is best accessed from marinas at Becher Bay or Pedder Bay.

Coastal trip

⌘◁〜↗ Port Renfrew – mile 0

There is beachfront camping along the mile of beach between the Gordon and San Juan Rivers. Although this area is typically sheltered from the swell of the open coast, the swell occasionally runs straight up Port San Juan and inundates the beach with large plunging surf. Stay at camp for another day and conditions will settle down. Departing from the beach, the western shore of Port San Juan to Botanical Beach Provincial Park is rocky with minimal opportunity to go ashore.

⌘↗ Botanical Beach Provincial Park – mile 5

Botanical Beach Provincial Park is located at the west entrance of Port San Juan. The shore is composed of flat sandstone and granite rock formations that have weathered to form tide pools filled with an extraordinary diversity marine life. Seastars, urchins, mussel, gooseneck barnacles, and sea anemones fill the pools with purple, red and orange green, blue and white. Some of the larger tide pools have been created by a granite boulder becoming trapped in a small pool and then, as wave action churns the boulder about, an every larger pool is ground out of the sandstone. The most striking rock formations are at the north end of the sandy beach where the weather has formed spectacular landscapes out of the soft sandstone. The area has been studied continuously since 1900 when it first came to the attention of biologists from the University of Minnesota.

Along areas of shelving rock you will need to be particularly aware and cautious of incoming waves. Periodically and a set of larger waves will arrive on shore breaking unpredictably, creating dangerous conditions. The two thousand resident species of marine life found here have adapted to contend with significant changes in temperature, salinity, and the high impact of storm waves.

The distance by road from the dock in Port Renfrew to the parking lot is 5 km. Allow 45 minutes on foot. Near the end the trail divides right to Botany Bay, and left for Botanical Beach.

⌘ Juan de Fuca Trail

The Juan de Fuca Trail runs 47 km (25 nmi) along the coast from Botanical Beach Provincial Park at the southeast entrance to Port San Juan to the trailhead at China Beach Provincial Park. The trail provides camping areas and

Chris Ladner leaving French Beach. Practice before doing this in a wilderness area.

A boulder beach such as Bear Beach is accessible in summer when the swell is less than 1 metre..

pit toilets strategically placed for hikers. The facilities along the trail are accessible and useful to sea kayakers.

The swell and surf along the shore diminishes as you progress east and come under the protection of the Olympic Peninsula. However, when swell height rises, surf conditions will be hazardous along shelving rocky shores and steep gravel beaches. The strong tidal currents running through Juan de Fuca Strait are intensified at the headlands, and tide rips can reach well out into the strait.

Providence Cove at approximatley mile 8 is a tiny inlet that is a popular lunch stop for hikers. It will be accessible on a calm day.

⌂ Kutshie Creek – mile 12

At Kutshie Creek there is a small sand and pea-gravel beach at the base of a small waterfall. Above the beach, at the east side of the creek there are established tent sites and pit toilets.

⌂⤢ Sombrio Beach – mile 15

This beach is a popular spot for camping, picnicing, and surfing. There is good road access with a parking lot at the end of short gravel road leading down from the coast highway. It is a 5 minute walk from the parking lot to the beach.

When the swell is more than a meter or two, the surf breaks large on the various aspects of Sombrio Beach. Some sections of the beach are very steep gravel and when the tide is high the surf is steep and plunging. The

Rum Running

Southern Vancouver Island is south of the 49th parallel of latitude, tucked into the crook of the Olympic Peninsula and adjacent to the San Juan Island of Washington State. It is less than a mile from Rum Island in the Canadian Gulf Islands to Turn Point in the American San Juan. In the 1920's, the United States prohibited the sale of alcohol, allowing ample opportunity for a profitable trade in illegal liquor from the shores of southern Vancouver Island.

Canadian smugglers ran contraband booze over to the San Juan Islands, the Olympic Peninsula and out through the Juan de Fuca Strait to points as far south as San Francisco. Under the cover of darkness heavily laden boats smuggled contraband booze to the alcohol impoverished citizens of a repressed nation. Johnny Schnarr was a Canadian folk hero with a $25,000 bounty on his head. With twin 860 horsepower motors, his powerful 56 foot-long armor-plated speed boat crossed the strait at 40 miles per hour. He would run 200 hundred cases of contraband liquor though a gauntlet of U.S. authorities equipped with machine guns, tracer bullets and four pound cannons.

⌂ Chin Creek – mile 19

Has sandy and gravel sections with good opportunities for camping. There is an established camping area with pit toilets at the western end of the beach. There is an emergency shelter sufficient to accommodate 4 persons well above the beach 250 metres east of the creek. The shelter was built before the park was created and should be used strictly for emergencies.

⌂ Bear Beach – mile 25

Is a shallow boulder beach with nice established camping on the west shore of the creek. Landing at Bear Beach is possible when the swell is very low.

⌂ Mystic Beach – mile 28

This low sandy beach has a moderate surf break. Watch for outcrops of rock. You will encounter people who have hiked the 2 km down from the southern trailhead of the Juan de Fuca Trail. The trailhead is 1 km east along the road from the China Beach campground and day-use area. Random camping is permitted on the beach.

⌘ China Beach – mile 30

is accessible from the highway by a 20 minute walk down a well maintained wide path. This beach is a very popular spot for day time hikers out for a picnic. The beach is ussually accessible thorough low but plunging surf. Wait for a lull between set of waves.

irregular shape of the shore offers the observant and careful paddler access through the larger waves. Surfers have used Sombrio Beach for decades and their presence is a good indication of where the surf is biggest. Excellent camping on wooden tent pallets is available on the west shore of the Sombrio River. There is also camping farther east along the beach.

⚓⊠ Jordan River Recreation Site – mile 21

This ia a popular kayak and surfing-boarding spot. Many local sea kayakers use this site for sharpening their skills. Situated well east into the Juan de Fuca Strait, the surf conditions at Jordan River vary by the day and by the hour. On days when swells do find their way in, the patterns of large and small set is very evident. Generally the river mouth is the easiest place to come ashore. In summer there is often no surf at all. If the surf is good there will be a lot of people on the water. There is small restaurant and a rustic shack from which great burgers are served to the surfing crowd.

⊠ Point No Point – mile 25

There are strong tidal currents close to the point and conditions can be rough with an ebb current running into a westerly wind.

⊠≋↗ French Beach Provincial Park – mile 28

The park has drive-in campsites within walking distance of the beach. Potable tapwater is available. The beach is steep and the surf plunges close to shore when the swell is high. French Beach is not fully exposed to the Pacific and during the summer is usually accessible by kayak. The west end of the beach away from the park is significantly flatter with softer surf. Summer conditions are usually calm.

⚓ Whiffin Spit – mile 35

A long spit of sand and gravel marks the entrance to Sooke Harbour. There is car access to the spit via Whiffin Spit Road off Sooke Road.

East of Whiffin Spit there are strong tidal currents close to Otter Point and Beechey Head. Conditions can be rough with an ebb current running into a westerly wind.

⚓◆ Sooke Harbour – mile 36

The entrance to Sooke Harbour is narrow with strong tidal currents. The middle of the channel can be rough when an ebb current flows against an incoming wind. Once inside, the harbour and inner basin are completely sheltered. The village of Sooke has full service and accommodation but no camping along its shore.

⌘ East Sooke Park

stretches along the shore from the east entrance to Sooke Harbour past Beechey Head. There is a large petroglyph etched into the rock less than a mile west of Beechy Head.

⊠≋↗⚓ Becher Bay – mile 41

Becher Bay has a marina with a boat launch and is a good point of access for day trips. Sea conditions can be rough when the current flows against wind along the shore between Becher Bay and Sooke.

⊠ Bentick Island – mile 43

is a Canadian military demolitions practice area with restricted access —no landing. The adjacent shore is used for naval underwater demolition practice—landing is not permitted. Signs are posted and security is present whenever the area is active.

⊠⌘ Race Rocks – mile 43

Race Passage between the dramatic black and white painted stone lighthouse and Vancouver Island is current swept and subject to quick changes in sea conditions and very rough tide rips. The current reference station indicates currents of 6 knots. However ththe station is 2 miles offshore. Near to Great Race Island the maximum currents will run closer to 9 knots; passage inside Bentick Island is much easier.

Race Rocks Ecological Reserve

Race Rocks is the most southerly part of Canada on the Pacific coast. It was established as an ecological reserve in 1980 to protect intertidal and subtidal life that thrives in the strong currents along these rocky shores.

The islands serve as a nesting site for gulls, cormorants, pigeon guillemots and oystercatchers. It is also a stopover for migratory birds. The birds share the rocks with harbour seals, sea lions and a few elephant seals. Transient killer whales pass near these shores looking for prey. Gray whales and Dall's and harbour porpoises are also visitors to the surrounding waters. There are accounts of over 100 shipwrecks along these rocky shores.

"No one ever questioned the need for a light on Race Rocks. Hudson's Bay Company officers bestowed that fitting title in 1842 as they watched the terrific eight- to ten-knot rip tides.

Scottish quarrymen sixteen thousand sea miles away, piecing together the tower at Race Rocks, cut and numbered each stone, stacked them in a ship's hold, and the tower made its way to Victoria as ballast. All through the hot spring and summer of 1860 the stones were wrestled up the ascending scaffolds and cemented into place." (from *Keepers of the Light*)

Race Rocks Lighthouse. Photo: Kevin Mansell.

◩♨ Pedder Bay – mile 46
Is completely sheltered with a full service marina, R.V. camping and a few tentsites in an open field.

⊠ William Head – mile 46
Stay well clear of William Head. It is the site of a Canadian Correctional Institution and any approach closer than a few hundred metres from shore will set of proximity alarms and bring prison guards down to the shore to send you away.

The shore from William Head to Victoria follows Coburg Spit which forms Esquimalt Lagoon and encloses the bird sanctuary.

Inside the lagoon Hatley Castle remains a sign of an aristocratic past. James Dunsmuir made part of his fortune mining BC coal. He commissioned the building of his home and ordered stone from Valdez and Saturna islands. He is quoted as saying: "Money doesn't matter, just build what I want." In 1908 the Dunsmuir family took up residence in Hatley Castle. In 1940 after the death of the last family member, the grounds were purchased by the Federal government for a military college and were sold again in 1995 to the BC Provincial Government to accommodate Royal Roads University.

⌘ Fisgard Lighthouse – mile 52
From here Fisgard Lighthouse should be in sight welcoming you back where the trip first began.

Short excursions

Saanich Inlet
Saanich Inlet is enclosed by the Saanich Peninsula extending north from Victoria. The peninsula encompasses the communities of Sidney, Brentwood Bay and Saanichton. The inlet is the only fjord inlet on Vancouver Island's east coast. Its steep southern slopes rise 335 metres to the highway above. The community of Brentwood

Bay, 15 miles north of Victoria along highway 17, provides principle access to the inlet. There is also a small marina on the western shore north of Goldstream Park.

Despite the encroachment of urban dwellings and past industrial development, the inlet retains a strong sense of wilderness. The sheltered waters are regularly visited by harbour seals, bald eagles, California sea lions and occasionally killer whales, stellar sea lions and osprey. There have been rare sightings of grey whales.

There is intermittent ship traffic in Saanich Inlet. Research and Coast Guard vessels travel in and out of Patricia Bay and occasionally freighters and military ships anchor in its sheltered waters. A small ferry runs 25 minutes across Sannich Inlet from Brentwood Bay to Mill Bay. Every once in a while a large BC Ferry will enter the inlet for training exercises or testing.

Sea planes operate north of the large jetty in Patricia Bay.

Paddling Conditions

Beginners will find ample adventure in Saanich Inlet, while intermediate paddlers can relax and take in the scenery of this bit of wilderness close to Vancouver Island's biggest city. On my first day in a sea kayak I paddled from Pat Bay to Brentwood Bay for lunch at a dockside restaurant. A 10 nmi round trip.

⌂◆ Brentwood Bay

The town of Brentwood Bay has full facilities and accommodation but no camping. There is parking and a canoe launch site adjacent to the BC Ferry terminal at the foot of Verdier Road. There is accommodation and restaurants right above the marina which also has kayak rentals.

Across Brentwood Bay, Tod Inlet runs 1 mile to an old limestone quarry that is now the world famous Buchart Gardens.

Tod Inlet has long been valued for its natural beauty and ecological significance. It now provides a safe and secluded overnight anchorage and marine access to the park.

⌘ Gowlland Tod Provincial Park

on the east shore of Saanich Inlet protects rare, dry coastal Douglas-fir habitat and is one of the last remaining natural areas in Greater Victoria. The 1,200 hectare park contains more than 40 kilometres of hiking trails.

⌘ McKenzie Bight

Farther south down Saanich Inlet, MacKenzie Bight has a nice beach providing shore access to the park's extensive hiking trails.

⌧ Squally Reach

On rare occasions wind at Squally Reach can rise rapidly to 40 knots after a fast-moving storm passes and the weather begins to improve. This is most likely to occur in early spring or late fall.

⌘⌂≋ Goldstream Provincial Park

The Goldstream estuary is at the southern end of the inlet and is a favoured feeding spot for Bald Eagles. From December to February Bald Eagles gather to feast on the carcasses of spawning salmon. The lower

The steep shores of Finlayson Arm are interupted by several small gravel beaches.

reaches of the estuary are closed to people and small boats. This protective measure has proven extremely effective. Since limiting access to the estuary, the number of wintering eagles has risen from a high of 12 to over 200.

Up the west side of the inlet is a gravel bar where Spectacle Creek reaches the sea in a small waterfall. Water levels in mid-summer can reduce the creek to a trickle but after a good rain the falls are picturesque.

Just north of Spectacle Creek you may notice a dozen stone steps leading nowhere; and a mile south, a partially built stone house that is now obscured by trees. Both were built as movie sets for the 1942 movie "Commandos Strike At Dawn" a WWII movie starring Paul Muni.

Although far from the realities of war, Saanich Inlet was chosen as the location because of its likeness to a Norwegian fjord.

⌘ Bamberton Cement works

This abandoned industrial site is obvious on the east shore of the inlet. The property was developed as a limestone quarry in 1913 and by the mid-1920s was a company town of several hundred people. The site included a school and community recreation facilities. Operation of the plant ceased in 1980 and the site was abandoned.

⌂⌇⌂ Bamberton Provincial Park

Bamberton Provincial Park is north of the old cement works. The campsites are too far from the beach to be accessed by kayaks, but could serve as a base camp for day trips. There is change house and washroom at the beach.

BC Ferries Mill Bay terminal is located a short distance north of Bamberton. The community of Mill Bay is nestled on the shore of the bay. From here it is 2.5 miles west across to Patricia Bay (known locally as Pat Bay).

⌘⚓ Patricia Bay
Pat Bay is the site of the Victoria International Airport, and the federal Institute of Ocean Sciences. The foreshore is a residential area and it is a very pleasant paddle south to Coles Bay Regional Park.

⌘⚓ Coles Bay Regional Park
Traditionally the Saanich first nations people spent winter in the protected waters of Coles Bay. There is a fine shallow beach facing the setting sun. Facilities in Coles Bay Regional Park include washrooms and picnic areas.

A nice spot to picnic where Spectacle Creek falls into Saanich Inlet.

Road Distances

How to use this chart

Mileages are cumulative across each column.

For example: to drive from Victoria to Toquart Bay, travel to Nanaimo (111 km) then to Port Alberni (84 km) then to Toquart Bay turn-off (100 km) and an additional 17 miles of gravel. Total distance 312 km.

Victoria

to Sidney			26 km
to Sooke			37 km
to Port Renfrew			107 km
to Duncan			60 km
	to Bamfield via Youbou		137 km (108 km gravel)
to Nanaimo			111 km
	to Port Alberni		84 km
		to Barkley Sound	3 hrs by ship
		to Ucluelet	4.5 hrs by ship
		to Bamfield	4.5 hrs by ship
		to Bamfield	95 km gravel
		to Toquart Bay turn-off	100 km (+17 km gravel)
to Tofino			316 km
to Campbell River			264 km
	to Goldriver		91 km
		to Friendly Cove	3 hrs by ship
		to Kyuquot	1-day by ship
	to Woss (a)		132 km
		to Zeballos	62 km gravel (b)
		to Fair Harbour	97 km gravel (b)
to Port McNeill			463 km
to Port Hardy			502 km
	to Holberg		42 km gravel (c)
	to Winter Harbour		76 km gravel (c)
	to Cape Scott		67 km gravel (c)

(a) Woss is evident only as a road entering the highway from the left and the gas station is out of sight 150 metres down the road. Stop and fuel-up and check your spare tire. Return to highway #19 and continue north.

(b) Distance is from the turn-off at highway #19, 20 km north of Woss.

(c) Distance is from the turn-off at highway #19 south of Port Hardy city limits.

On gravel roads consider an approximate average speed of 40 km per hour.
On paved highways consider 65 km per hour average.

First Nations Contacts

The following is a list of the First Nations Band offices along the shores of Vancouver Island. Contact the appropriate band office for information on camping on Reserve land and First Nations commercial campgrounds.

First Nations	Geographic area	Area code (250)
Nanoose	Nanoose Bay	390-3661
Qualicum	Qualicum Beach	757-9337
K'ómoks Nation	Comox	339-4545
Wei Wai Kai	Quadra Island	285-3316
Wei Wai Kum	Campbell River	286-6949
Namgis	Alert Bay	974-5556
Kwakiutl Band Council	Port Hardy	949-6012
Gwa'sala-'Nakwaxda'xw Nation	Port Hardy	949-8343
Tlatlasikwala Band	Nawhitti	949-5751
Quatsino	Quatsino Sound	949-6245
Nuu-chah-nulth Tribal Council	Vanc. Is. west Coast	724-5757
Uchucklesaht	Uchucklesaht Inlet	724-1832
Ka:'yu:'k't'h'/Che:k'tles7et'h	Kyuquot Sound	332-5259
Ehattesaht	Zeballos	761-4155
Nuchatlaht	Nootka Island	724-8609
Mowachaht / Muchalaht	Nootka Sound	283-2015
Hesquiaht	Hesquiat Harbour	670-1100
Ahousaht	Vargas & Meares Island	670-9563
		670-9531
Tla-o-qui-aht	Clayoquot Sound	725-3233
		1-800-883-7707
Ucluelet	Ucluelet	726-7342
Toquaht	Toquart Bay	726-4230
		1-877-726-4230
Tseshaht	Broken Islands	724-1225
		1-888-724-1225
Huu-ay-aht	Northern West Coast Trail Bamfield	1-888-644-4555
Ditidaht	Central West Coast Trail	745-3333
Pacheedaht	Pachena West Coast Trail	1-888-231-1110

Additional Reading

Reference

Government of Canada. Ministry of Fisheries and Oceans. *Current Atlas: Juan de Fuca Strait to Strait of Georgia.* 1999.

Government of Canada. Ministry of Fisheries and Oceans. *Sailing Directions: British Columbia Coast (southern portion).* 2003.

Government of Canada. Ministry of Fisheries and Oceans. *Small Craft Guide* vol 1, 15th edition 1990

Mussio, *Backroads Mapbook* 3rd edition. Mussio Ventures Ltd. New West Minister BC. 2001.

General Sea Kayaking

Alderson, Douglas. *Sea Kayaker's Savvy Paddler: more than 500 Tips for Better Paddling.* Camden ME: ragged Mountain Press, 2001

Foster, Nigel. *Surf Kayaking.* Guilford, Connecticut: The Globe Pequot Press, 1998.

Hanson, Jonathan. *Complete Sea Kayak Touring.* Camden, Maine: Ragged Mountain Press, 1998.

Hutchison, Derek. *The Complete Book of Sea Kayaking.* Guilford, Connecticut: The Globe Pequot Press, 1995.

Johnson, Shelley. *The Complete Sea Kayaker's Handbook.* Camden Maine: Ragged Mountain Press, 2002.

Seidman, David. *The Essential Sea Kayaker.* Camden, Maine: Ragged Mountain Press, 2001.

Navigation

Birch, David. *Fundamentals of Kayak Navigation.* Guilford Connecticut: Globe Pequot, 1999.

Eyges, Leonard. *The Practical Pilot: Coastal Navigation by Eye, Intuition, and Common Sense.* Camden, Maine: International Marine Publishing, 1989.

Lethem, Lawrenc. *GPS Made Easy* 4th edition. Calgary. Rocky Mountain Books. 2003

Moyer, Lee. *Sea Kayak Navigation Simplified.* Mukilteo, Washington: Alpen Books Press, 2001

Wing, Charlie. *Boating Magazines One Minute Guide to the Nautical Rules of the Road.* Camden, Maine: International Marine/ Ragged Mountain Press, 1998

Environment

West Coast Marine Weather Hazards Manual. Environment Canada and Gordon Soules Publishing, 1992.

Lange, Owen, S. Living With Weather. Canada: Environment Canada. 2003.

Lange, Owen S. *The Wind Came All Ways: a quest to understanding the winds, waves and weather in the Georgia Basin.* Canada: Department of Fisheries and Oceans, 1998.

Thomson, Richard. *Oceanography of the British Columbia Coast.* Canada: Department of Fisheries and Oceans, 1981.

Safety and Rescue

Alderson, Douglas and Pardy, Michael. *Sea Kayaker Magazines Handbook of Safety and Rescue.* Camden, Maine: Ragged Mountain Press, 2003.

Broze, Matt and George Gronseth. *Sea Kayaker Deep Trouble: True Stories and Their Lessons from Sea Kayaker Magazine.* Camden, Maine: International Marine/Ragged Mountain Press, 1997.

Lull, John. *Sea Kayaking Safety and Rescue.* Berkeley, California: Wilderness Press, 2001.

Schumann, Roger and Jan Shriner. *Sea Kayak Rescue: The Definitive Guide to Modern Reentry and Recovery Techniques.* Guilford, Connecticut: The Globe Pequot Press, 2001.

First aid

Christensen, Anna. *Mis*Adventure: Rise To The Challenge.* Pub Wilderness Alert. 2003Vancouver BC. 2003

Isaac, Jeffrey. *The Outward Bound Wilderness First-Aid Handbook.* New York, New York: The Lyons Press, 1998.

National Safety Council and Wilderness Medical Society. *Wilderness First Aid: Emergency Care for Remote Locations.* Sudbury, Massachusetts: Jones and Bartlett Publishers, 1998.

Travel and adventure

Blades, Michael. *Day Of Two Sunsets.* Victoria, BC.Orca Books. 1993.

Coffey, Maria et al. *Sailing Back in Time: A Nostalgic Voyage on Canada's West Coast.* Vancouver BC. Whitecap Books. 1996.

Streetly, Joanna. *Paddling Through Time.* Vancouver BC.Raincoast Books. 2000.

Voss, Captain John. *The Venturesome Voyages of Captain Voss.* Sidney BC. Gray's Publishing. 1976.

Ecology

Carefoot, Thomas. *Pacific Seashores.* Vancouver, BC. J.J. Douglas Ltd. 1977.

Ludvigsen, Rolf & Beard, Graham. *West Coast Fossils: a guide to the ancient life of Vancouver Island.* Vancouver BC. Whitecapp Books. 1994.

Smith, Ian. *The Unknown Island.* J.J. Douglas Ltd. 1973.

Snively, Gloria. *Exploring the Seashore.* Vancouver, BC.Gordon Soules Book Publishers. 1978.

History

Graham, David. *Lights of the Inside Passage.* Maderia Park BC. Harbour Publishing. 1986.

Graham, David. *Keepers of the Light.* Maderia Park BC. Harbour Publishing. 1985.

Harboard, Heather. *Nootka Sound and the Surrounding Waters of Maquinna.* Surrey, BC. Heritage House Publishing Company Limited, 1996.

Hoover, Alan. *Nuu-chah-nulth Voices: Histories, Objects and Journeys.* UNI-presses. 2000.

Horsfield, Margaret, *Cougar Annie's Garden.* Salal Books. 1999.

Jewitt, John. White Slaves of Maquinna: Jewitt's narrative of capture and confinement at Nootka. Victoria BC. Heritage House. 2000.

Koppel, Tom. *Kanaka.* Vancouver BC. Whitecap. 1995

Nicholson, George. *Vancouver Island's West Coast.*Vancouver, BC. George Nicholson's Books. 1965.

Parker, Marion and Tyrell, Robert. *Rumrunner.* Victoria, BC. Orca Book Publishers. 1988.

Peterson, Lester R. *The Cape Scott Story.* Vancouver, BC. Mitchell Press. 1974.

Rogers, Fred. *Shipwrecks of British Columbia.* Vancouver, BC. Douglas & McIntyre. 1973

Scott, R. Bruce. *Breakers Ahead.* Victoria, BC. Fleming Review Printing. 1970

Scott, R. Bruce. Barkley Sound: a history of the Pacific Rim National Park area. Victoria, BC. Fleming Review Printing. 1970.

Scott, R. Bruce. *Peoples of Southwest Coast of Vancouver Island.* Victoria, BC.

Websites

The following list of website includes government and regional sites that provide an abundance of links to the widest variety of services. A few specific sites are provided where their services are of particular value in an area.

- Alert Bay Tourism http://www.alertbay.com/tourism.htm
- BC Provincial Parks http://wlapwww.gov.bc.ca/bcparks
- BC Parks campsite reservations & hours/dates of operation. http://www.discovercamping.ca/
- BC Ferries routes, schedules, rates, reservations. http://www.bcferries.bc.ca
- Catala Charters (Port Hardy) – Accomodations, water taxis – God's Pocket and Cape Scott http://www.catalacharters.net/
- Denman Island Welcomes You! http://www.denmanisland.com/
- God's Pocket Resort http://www.godspocket.com/
- Hornby island's community web http://www.hornbyisland.net/
- Interactive maps, parks, trails, and camping. This is an e cellent site with extensive links to all communities and activities. http://www.britishcolumbia.com
- Lady Rose Marine Services & Sechart Lodge. Transportation between Port Alberni and Barkley Sound. Accomodation at Sechart Lodge. http://www.ladyrosemarine.com/
- Nootka Sound water taxi and services http://www.ferrercharters.com/
- North Island Kayak rentals and tours. Telegraph Cove and Port Hardy. http://www.kayakbc.ca/
- Pachena Bay Campground – west coast trail http://www.huuayaht.ca/pachena/
- Parks Canada –Pacific Rim National Park - West coast trail http://www.pc.gc.ca
- Rainforest Kayak Adventures – guides, trips, courses. http://www.rainforestkayak.com/
- Remote Passages – Tofino, kayak tours, guides, information. http://www.remotepassages.com
- Tofino Sea Kayaking Company and the Paddlers Inn. http://www.tofino-kayaking.com/index.html
- Vancouver Island North Visitors Association – accomdations and services. http://www.tourismni.com/vinva/
- Vancouver Island Parks http://www.vancouverislandparks.com/
- Vancouver Island excellent site for communities, maps, accomodation and services. http://www.vancouverisland.com/
- Vancouver Island accommodation, travel, tourism directory. http://www.vancouverislandaccommodations.com
- Vancouver island & the gulf islands www.visit-vancouverisland.com

Index